Ricky Reel: Silence is not an option

Ricky Reel:
Silence is not
an option

Sukhdev Reel

Ricky Reel: Silence Is Not An Option
by Sukhdev Reel

First edition published by Bookmarks in 2022
© Bookmarks Publications Ltd
c/o 1 Bloomsbury Street, London WC1B 3QE
www.bookmarksbookshop.co.uk

ISBN 978-1-914143-57-1 paperback
ISBN 978-1-914143-58-8 Kindle
ISBN 978-1-914143-59-5 epub
ISBN 978-1-914143-60-1 pdf

Typeset by Colm Bryce & Simon Guy
for Bookmarks Publications
Cover design by Ben Windsor
Cover photograph by Guy Smallman
Printed by Halstan & Co Ltd, Amersham, England

Contents

Acknowledgments

Thank you.

To my husband who continues to support me during this painful journey: two souls who are hurting but continue to support each other. For always being the person I could turn to during those dark and desperate times. He sustained me in ways that I never knew I needed.

To my children and grandchildren. I am sorry I neglected you sometimes, but your strength and determination to find how your brother and uncle died gave me courage to become a campaigner to seek justice. Fly high fearlessly and don't let anyone clip your wings. Have the courage to fight injustices. Always remember you should neither commit injustice against another nor suffer injustice yourself.

The story of this fight started with the assistance and support of John McDonnell, Suresh Grover and Mon Matharu, later joined by Mike Schwarz. Thank you for continuing to support me through this journey. I do not think I'd be alive today without your support. I value the insight, guidance, assistance and wisdom you provide in fighting for justice for Ricky.

Your support and encouragement over the years has made me more determined to find out how my son met his death. No matter what, you have always been there for me, giving me encouragement when I felt all doors were closed to me. Thank you also to all the members of the Southall Monitoring Group, now known as The

Monitoring Group, especially Jagdish Patel and Ammy Phull for taking photographs at our events. It is good to have these people supporting my family when challenging different authorities. They also did a lot of publicity events without which the campaign would not have travelled all over the world

To hundreds of my supporters, who are too numerous to mention. You all know who you are as you make contact with me regularly to offer support. My sincere thanks and appreciation for taking the time to contact me and to support and highlight Ricky's case. I appreciate all of you taking the time to send me encouraging messages. These feel like incredible gifts and blessings and also a bright spot in my dark days. Even after 25 years, the warmth of those who care has brought us very real comfort; we appreciate the way you faithfully continue to reach out to us. So now I share my story with you all.

To Michael Mansfield who supported us through the most difficult phase of the campaign. His brilliant mind managed to overturn the verdict which was planned for us. Your dedication and understanding mean a lot to my family. Thank you for achieving some sort of justice for Ricky on the day when the whole world seemed like a hostile, cold and empty place. I am honoured to call you a friend.

To Louise Christian and Sadiq Khan for dealing with our case. As I challenged the many institutions, it was brilliant to have you in my corner advising me and showing me how to deal with the many obstacles placed in my way

Writing this book was harder than I thought because I had to relive the trauma, not that I have ever forgotten it. None of this would have been possible without my friends Dave Smith and Phil Chamberlain, who encouraged me to write this book, together with their generosity and support all along the way. It is because of their efforts and encouragement that I have Ricky's legacy to pass on to my family and the world.

To Bruce McDonald, former CEO of Kingston upon Thames, now a Lib Dem leader of Elmbridge. Thank you for being a friend, supporting our campaign and arranging five memorial lectures for Ricky in Kingston. Also thank you to all the speakers: Mr Michael Mansfield QC, Mr John McDonnell MP, Mr Imran Khan QC, Dr Richard Stone, panel member of the Stephen Lawrence Inquiry, and Ms Yasmin Alibhai-Brown, a journalist and an author.

To all the music producers, directors, songwriters and singers for highlighting my son's plight through music. To Benjamin Zephaniah and Mac Rogers for their beautiful poem and ballad for Ricky.

To Hugh Goodacre and Su Goodacre for arranging several meetings and supporting my young son years ago by buying him a "Yo-Yo" and playing with him.

To Elaine Richardson and family for supporting my whole family and raising Ricky's case throughout the country, attending several meetings with trade unions and other organisations. Looked after my children when I was unable to due to travelling to raise the profile of this case.

To the late Linda Chapman, for assisting us with Ricky's case. Always ready to lend a hand.

To all my friends and colleagues at LB Hounslow for marching with me, supporting me and staying with me till now. Anthony, Prakash, Farah, Elaine and Zarayna accompanied us, marching the streets of Kingston day and night searching for Ricky together with hundreds of people.

To all the trade unions, shop stewards, the Blacklist Support Group, the Campaign Opposing Police Surveillance, the Undercover Research Group, Police Spies Out of Lives, the Socialist Workers Party, all the politicians who supported us and everybody who has contributed in any way they could to support the Justice for Ricky Reel Campaign. Please know that we are thankful for your support.

To everybody else who signed our petitions, attended conferences and meetings, highlighted our campaign and supported us during this very difficult time of our lives. To journalists from TV and other media channels for highlighting our plight for justice.

To all gurdwaras, temples, mandirs, mosques, churches and all other organisations supporting this campaign.

To Mukesh Solanki for printing Ricky Reel t-shirts.

To Saffron Burrows for marching the many demonstrations with me.

To Rob Morgan for printing our brochures and to Neil Armstrong for supporting and creating a lot of publicity for the campaign

To Tony Staunton and Jon McKenzie for arranging several events in Plymouth including the Civil Rights Caravan in Plymouth which later travelled to Prague.

To Liz for arranging many events in Scotland including tying yellow ribbons all over Scotland.

To Shaista and Ushma for support and arranging many concerts including designing and producing the KEEP IT REEL CD with Sanj, ADF, Coco, and performers.

To Tommy Nagra for supporting our campaign and also highlighting our case by producing a documentary and staged a reconstruction. He did what the police failed to do.

To Rishi Rich, Kiranee, Ameet Chana and Raj Ghai for creating the "Justice for Ricky Reel" song showing our fight full of pain to the world: youtu.be/ry6xEAHwE1I.

To Farah for feeding my children in my absence. Their "pizza lady".

To Guy Smallman for the cover photo and his patience in doing so. To Ben Windsor for the beautiful design of the cover and the book. To Jess Hurd, Denis Fernando and Gary Calton for allowing us to use their lovely photographs. For the legal team—taking on authorities is not easy. But thank you for support and having you with me to fight my corner.

To Colm Bryce, Simon Guy and Carol Williams for turning this manuscript into a book and making my dream of writing a book come true. A dream I had for years finally turned into reality. I will always remember Colm's faith in me and his words which made me decide that no other publisher will publish my book except him. He said "I will treat your book with all the dignity it deserves", without even looking at the manuscript. I am glad to say that he has kept that promise. No other words greater than this for a mother who has put her life on hold to get justice for her son. I am honoured to call him a dear friend.

To Halstan & Co Ltd for printing my book, together with everybody else who has contributed towards it.

Sukhdev Reel
May 2022

Photo by Jess Hurd

Ricky Reel: Silence is not an Option

Introduction

John McDonnell MP

I am the Reel family's local Member of Parliament. I have known Mr and Mrs Reel and their children for years. So when Ricky went missing and they needed help it was natural that they contacted me.

I have worked for decades with Suresh Grover and the Monitoring Group, dealing with case after case of miscarriages of justice and participating with him in local and national anti-racist campaigns.

Similarly, Anthony Way and I have worked together in our local community in Hayes throughout the time he was a local councillor and was a work colleague of Sukhdev Reel.

Within the first 24 hours of Ricky not returning home, the family, Suresh and Anthony contacted me because they were desperately worried that, completely out of character, Ricky had not returned home from a night out with his friends and had not been in contact with his family.

They all instinctively knew that something was seriously wrong. The reason they contacted me was because no matter how hard they tried they could not get the police to take their fears seriously.

All they were asking the police for was a thorough search and investigation to find Ricky and discover what had happened to keep him out of touch. I did what any local MP would do and contacted my local Police Commander to seek urgent assistance from the police to find Ricky.

From then on and for the next two decades we witnessed a complete failure of our justice system to secure justice for the Reel family, a system which continues to fail the family.

Although from the outset I hoped that our local police team in Hillingdon had appreciated the seriousness of the situation, Ricky went missing in another Met Police division in Kingston upon Thames and the responses from the police there clearly demonstrated that they did not.

It's widely understood that the first 24 to 48 hours of any incident or crime or missing person inquiry are critical to any investigation to discover what has happened.

The first 24 to 48 hours in this case were chaotic with the police response lacking judgement, basic professionalism, resources and indeed empathy or cultural awareness.

This was the pattern of the police behaviour from here on. From the first day, the onus for discovering the truth of what happened to Ricky has fallen on the family at every stage.

It has been the family that has had to undertake its own investigation from day one, even initially having to undertake basic investigatory work to trace Ricky's body and the events in Kingston upon Thames on the night he went missing.

The family found from the beginning that their views didn't seem to count to the police.

They felt profoundly disrespected.

The investigation has been a catalogue of basic errors and incompetence followed by what can only be described as an institutional resistance to accountability, exemplified throughout.

Just at the time when Ricky's family were appealing for more policing resources to be devoted to the investigation of what happened to Ricky, we discovered that there were police being deployed but that they were deployed in surveillance of our campaign.

A whole new vocabulary has been invented by the policing strategy of spy cops.

We were told years later that this was "collateral intrusion".

An obsessive secrecy and the obdurate refusal to be open with the family resulted in me at one point having to use Parliamentary privilege to simply get into the public domain the findings of a supposedly independent investigation into the handling of this case by the police.

At times the lack of openness and transparency was farcical and at other times tragically sad.

The use of the redaction of reports provided to the family and me by the police rendered them farcical at times as only individual words were revealed and we were not allowed to take away our individual copies in case we put them together to make sense of sentences.

The distress caused was immense when on another occasion the family read in a national newspaper the intimate details of what was done to Ricky's body in post-mortems that the family were not consulted on or even made aware of by the police.

The family and the campaigners supporting us should also not have had to live in fear of arrest for simply demanding access to information on what the police knew and what their failings were in the investigation.

Many believe that the treatment of the Reel family with such disrespect evidenced the continuing institutional racism of the Metropolitan Police.

If it wasn't for the courage and determination of Sukhdev Reel and her family and the commitment of the campaigners and advisers, like Suresh Grover, the loss of Ricky Reel would have become just another unsolved case file on the shelves of Scotland Yard.

It is heartrending for any mother to lose their child but this is made so much worse when it is not known how this loss occurred.

All the Reel family have ever wanted is the truth and justice.

They and all of us who have supported them will not rest until we have secured the truth about what happened to Ricky and secured justice for him and his family.

John McDonnell MP
March 2022

Sukhdev Reel: a loving mother and a fearless campaigner
Suresh Grover

As soon as I met Sukhdev Reel on Thursday 16 October 1997, a couple of days after her beloved son was reported missing, I was struck by her honesty, her care for her children and her single, focused determination to initially find him and then seek justice in his name. Some of these qualities continue to radiate in the public in her endeavour to raise her son's plight nationally and internationally. Others, such as her bravery, have overcome most of the insidious obstacles thrown by the state in her path ostensibly to defeat the family-led campaign that has managed to prevail over a quarter of century.

Only one outcome still remains beyond her reach—justice, a result almost impossible to attain in our society where the values and practice of the justice system are pitted against all working-class people and especially its Black and Asian constituents.

It was the realisation by the family of the existence of this structural obstacle that led the family and us to collectively to form the Campaign in Ricky Reel's name. Sukhdev wasn't just simply confronting individual prejudice but an institution that was failing her and her peers because of her class, race and sex. From then on, for her and her family, meetings, interviews and protests became as common as hot meals and haircuts.

Sukhdev knew that I was constantly involved coordinating other high-profile campaigns, she joined their meetings, she marched with them, shared their tears and pain and encouraged them not to give up. It is her character that drove Neville Lawrence, Stephen's father to support her campaign and a close bond formed between them.

How did the state respond? Rather than learn lessons, it shamefully began to spy on her and the campaign by deploying undercover SDS police officers. She is now a core participant at the Undercover Police 'Spycops' Inquiry, established to examine police spying of peaceful protest groups.

The crisis in policing that led them to be officially and legally deemed as institutionally racist in 1999 has only worsened.

Last year, the nation was again shocked when a police officer staged a fake Covid arrest, forcibly kidnapped, raped and brutally murdered a young woman, Sara Everard.

An official Independent Panel examining the murder of private detective Daniel Morgan concluded that 'Metropolitan Police was institutionally corrupt'. The state narrative and criminalisation of black youth by the use of a 'Gangs Matrix' has been exposed as racist.

Amnesty International has described the Matrix as "a racially discriminatory system that stigmatises young black men for the music they listen to or their behaviour on social media". It warned: "Some police officers have been acting like they're in the Wild West, making the false assumption that they can set up fake profiles and covertly befriend people online to monitor them".

In its editorial of 10 July 2020, *The Guardian* pleaded with the Met commissioner "to police people and do not terrorise them".

Sukhdev's threat to the state is simply daring to challenge and to make her beloved son's cause prominent in public eye. Over the last 25 years, Sukhdev has met activists, lawyers, family justice campaigners, poets, writers and musicians who have become her friends. She is a mother warrior who inspires others around her. That is her only crime.

Suresh Grover
May 2022

Suresh Grover (left) at the Ricky Reel Memorial Lecture, Kingston upon Thames, 2002

Suresh is founder of The Monitoring Group and has coordinated many family-led justice campaigns including those linked to the killing of Stephen Lawrence, Zahid Mubarek and Victoria Climbie

Reason for writing a book

The reason I have written this book is:

1. To introduce Ricky to his nieces and nephews who unfortunately did not have the opportunity to meet him. How he would have loved them! They know about him and what happened to him. Some are too young to know or understand but one day they will.

2. People have shown a lot of interest in Ricky's life and his case. I thought this book would answer some of the questions about Ricky's case and family.

3. To show Ricky's killers how much damage they have caused to my family and our lives. We are waiting for you to speak up, maybe you are also struggling with your conscience.

4. I hope this book will allow those people who find it so hard to understand why we continue to fight for justice to get an insight into what it is to lose someone you love so much to such a pointless notion as racism. The reason I continue to fight is

not to exact revenge or retribution—it is for a reason far more humane than this. I want to stop families being ripped apart in the way ours has and to stop the senseless hatred which has become a norm in our society. I do not bear a grudge against anyone because Ricky's love would not permit me to do so. He led a peaceful and happy life. I simply want to know how and why my son died.

By a mother in pain.

Sukhdev Reel
April 2022

Chapter 1

Ricky is missing, Ricky is found

A child is a gift so precious and pure
A life joined to your life in ways you can't see
The day you were born was so full and perfect
The day you left was timeless, hopeless and empty

"We have found your son's body in the river Thames in Kingston", said the police.

As I heard these words, a big black hole opened and engulfed me. I fought for breath and I tried to climb out big black clouds that were floating around me. Warm air surrounded me and I felt arms embrace my body. Could this just be a bad dream ?

This was on 21 October 1997, a date that represented the absolute end of "normal life" for our family.

My legs turned to jelly, refusing to hold me up. My husband—Ricky's father, Balwant, was shaking as he helped me get up. I tried saying something to comfort him, but no words came.

Engulfed again I could not see, hear or think beyond the vortex. My body went from boiling hot, to an icy cold. Then somebody grabbed my hand. I tried to open my eyes but could not do it. Then I heard Ricky's voice reassuring me, "I'm with you mum". I thought to myself, in my head and not out loud, that the police must have pulled somebody else from the river. It could not be him.

I felt someone shaking me, calling my name and telling me to open my eyes. I wanted to stay in situ, never to wake again.

I was told I collapsed upon hearing Ricky was dead. My eyes were lead-heavy as I woke up on the cold floor.

I touched my scarf. Bulldozed. Baffled. Blindsided. I was still wearing the scarf which Ricky liked and which was a symbol of his safe return to me. I had worn it every day I went looking for him during the week he was missing, the days before I heard these terrible words. My mother told me to keep something he had given me close. Perhaps to comfort me, and to keep the hope of finding him alive.

That morning, before I heard those life shattering words, I had gone to the offices of Southall Monitoring Group (SMG) to deliver a media appeal through a press conference for witnesses to my 20 year old son's disappearance a week earlier on 14 October 1997. My desperation to find Ricky prepared me to do anything and everything to bring him home safely. I left that office without even getting to make that plea that day because the news of his death was delivered to me before the press conference even began.

But let me go back, and tell you how this terrible ordeal had first begun, seven days earlier when my Ricky was alive and well and life was "normal".

Exactly one week earlier, on 14 October 1997, Ricky had decided on have a rare night out. He had telephoned to tell me not to cook for him that night—though I had already done so. I was going out with my younger son to an open evening at his school and was busy rushing around to get ready.

This was a rare night out for Ricky, who was doing a placement year during his Computer Science degree at Brunel. He wanted to celebrate a friend's birthday and would be back by 1.00 am. I was happy he was finally going out instead of spending the whole time on his computer, helping his family, etc. I was not worried, knowing if Ricky said he'd be back at 1.00am, he would be back at 1.00am. His particular timekeeping was something I always joked about: "with Ricky around, I never need a watch!"

The instant he failed to phone to say he would be late; I knew he was in some kind of trouble. Call it a mother's instinct. A lot of parents have that—the blessing and curse of intuition.

He and his three friends were travelling in Dean's car, so I started phoning police stations and hospitals in case they had been involved in an accident.

My children have always been aware of my habit of waiting until everyone is home before relaxing. They know I will not go to bed before they get home and they understand it is a fear which started when I suffered a tragedy. I am not a "clinging" mother, but like most, have always slept better with all the family safely under the same roof. I no longer sleep well now, even when all the other children are at home because one is still missing and my heart aches for him to return home so that I can finally go to sleep.

On 14 October 1997 I spent the entire night sitting on the stairs waiting for Ricky. This absence was totally out of his character. My other children woke up wanting to know why I was not in bed. I told them I was waiting for Ricky and they should sleep because of school in the morning.

I continued to telephone various police stations and hospitals to ascertain whether anyone had reported a car accident with four Asian boys in it. At the same time, I prayed for everybody's safe return. At 3.00am I felt somebody was calling me and needed my help. I must have dozed off on the stairs for a few minutes when a current ran through my body and pierced my heart. I had experienced nothing like this before, nor since. Frightened and convinced Ricky needed my help, I rang his mobile repeatedly, but calls went immediately to voicemail. The night passed at a painfully slow pace while I prayed for Ricky's safety. In the morning I telephoned my local police station at West Drayton requesting help to find my son.

I was told that as he was over 18, I would have to wait for 24 hours as per the Police Missing Persons Policy and to contact them if he did not return home. I explained Ricky had never gone missing before and told her what he was like, how worried I was and after much persuasion and a lengthy conversation, the duty officer reluctantly agreed to send a police officer to my home, but she did not give a precise time. Meanwhile, the clock on Ricky's disappearance kept ticking.

That morning I sent my two children to school thinking it would distract them from all the chaos in the household, plus I was not in a fit state to look after them or able to answer their questions about their brother. My focus at this time was to telephone anyone who could help us. My youngest son was only 11 years old. He needed to be spared any distress because he also wanted to know why his big brother was not at home. I was sure that Ricky would come home, albeit hurt or injured, whilst simultaneously shielding my children from any shock. Unbeknown to me that one day in my absence they would be dealt the worst possible blow from which they would not recover.

I telephoned my elder brother Mon, and briefly explained about Ricky and asked him to come to our house urgently, we were lost, needed support, someone to talk to who could show us a way forward. Ricky was very close to Mon.

I phoned my work and told them I could not go in, then sat on a chair near the living room window so that I could see when the police arrived. Reeling and restless, I wanted to stand up and walk around the room but couldn't stop my body from shaking.

I telephoned the Security office at Brunel University where the party was to find out whether there had been any disturbances during the previous night's event. I asked if he could trace Ricky's friends or give me their phone numbers so I could speak to the people who were out with him. He said he was not aware of any disturbances and refused to give me anyone's number as it was against their policy. All I could do was give him my telephone number to pass on to anyone who knew Ricky.

After an hour I telephoned the local police station again and explained I was very anxious and frightened and needed to speak to someone as I was still waiting for a police officer to visit the house. The female on the phone shouted that an officer had visited my home, but I had not opened the door to him. I told her no police officer had visited and explained I would have seen anyone coming to the door as I had been waiting at the window. She began arguing and refused to listen to me and said I was wasting vital police resources and time by not opening the door. I pleaded with her that I was worried and needed help locating my son. Finally, she said she would send an officer.

A few minutes later a police officer came to my house and apologised that he had gone to the wrong address earlier. Though he listened to my concerns about Ricky, he repeated the missing person's policy and was unable to help. I told him to ring the Security office at Brunel who might provide police telephone details of Ricky's friends. Sure enough, after speaking to a security officer, he spoke to one of Ricky's friends, who, though he was not out with the group of them that night, could provide telephone numbers of those who were.

The police officer called Dean, who advised that the four of them had changed their minds at the last moment, deciding to go to Kingston upon Thames instead of Brunel University.

As they were walking into the town centre after parking Dean's car in Down Hall Road, two men nearby started shouting racial abuse at Ricky and his friends. This later turned into an altercation where the men had attacked them.

Dean said everybody ran away in different directions to get away from this attack. Three of the four regrouped. Ricky was not seen again.

Dean said that just before the attack Ricky was talking about going home as he had promised to be back by 1.00 am and also because he was due to attend a Microsoft Conference in London early next day.

The friends went to Options Nightclub thinking Ricky had gone home after the attack. We asked his friends to come to our house as we needed to talk to them because Ricky was still missing, and his jacket and mobile were still in Dean's car.

I phoned Ricky's employers to advise of the past evening's events. ID was required for this meeting, as well as paperwork which was still in his room on his bed—together with his shirt and suit ready for the meeting in the morning. He had this habit of getting everything ready the night before so that he didn't have to rush in the morning. I showed Ricky's room to the police officer.

Mon came and we waited for Ricky's friends to arrive. It took them a long time. Only two friends instead of three arrived at lunchtime and Mon, Balwant, Maneet and Dean (Ricky's friends) went to Kingston.

Down Hall Road in Kingston upon Thames, as it looked in 1997. This is where Ricky and his friends parked their car

The friends retraced their steps showing us what they did that night. They had bought alcohol from a shop and had parked their car on Down Hall Road where they had a few drinks. They asked directions to Options Nightclub from a passing police car.

In those days Down Hall Road was quite desolate. It had some derelict buildings and lots of shrubs. The friends told us they had all urinated near the car and the fence. It was a dark and deserted road. The river was at one end of the road with a light and sign saying DEEP WATER— there was a big park at the end of the road next to the sign.

Balwant, Mon, Dean and Maneet went on to Kingston police station while I remained at home, hoping and praying.

The spot on the River Thames where Ricky is believed to have entered the water

A police officer in Kingston rattled out the "24 hour" ritual despite being told in clear terms how the four boys had been attacked. He then stated many reasons Ricky might be missing: (a) he might not want to be found, (b) he might have run away as we, his parents might be trying to force him into an arranged marriage as is common with Asian people, (c) he said with a wink that unknown to us our son could be gay, and decided to run away to pursue this life.

This man assumed that my family had caused Ricky's disappearance, a new version of blaming the victim. Balwant and Mon were stunned by the attitude of this "law enforcer". Mon told him that The Options Nightclub's manager informed them of an Asian gig that night, to which the police were called, due to a "few scuffles".

Mon asked if there were any arrests and could they see if Ricky was one of those caught in the scuffle. The police officer reluctantly went down to check the cells, returning to confirm Ricky was not among the people arrested that night.

I knew then with a sinking heart after dealing with the police from West Drayton and Kingston that they were not interested in helping us. We were just confused and frightened parents, with no idea how to make the police understand how much we needed their help to find our son.

We needed someone to guide us, to be our voice, a voice that would not be ignored the way our voices had been.

We needed authorities to take note of the racial nature of the attack, which the victims had reported to the police. We needed them to understand Ricky had never failed to come home before. We needed them to identify a parents' fear that their son might never ever return home.

I remembered Mr Suresh Grover, director of the Southall Monitoring Group a community based anti-racist organisation in West London. We first met when I worked at the Housing Department of a local authority in Greater London.

My department dealt with people and families who faced homelessness. Not only would we deal with their homeless situation but many other associated (often complex) problems and needs.

One day Suresh brought a client in who was fleeing domestic violence. I was on duty and interviewed the client while Suresh stayed outside. The way he helped my client impressed me. I later found out about the services offered by the Southall Monitoring Group. Had the police listened and believed me there would have been no reason to look for someone else to assist me to find my son.

Family and friends continued to telephone for any updates. My eldest daughter was at a University outside London. Her friend brought her home.

I telephoned Suresh on 15 October 1997 and left a message to contact me urgently. This turned out to be one of the best decisions I could have made. It was this telephone call that turned us from a family grieving to a grieving family fighting for justice.

Suresh and his team have been some of my family's greatest allies, as has John McDonnell, my MP. I had dealt with MPs in a professional capacity only, at work. Suresh and his colleagues from the Southall Monitoring Group came to see me on 16 October 1997 and discussed the case and offered help. Suresh then left by saying he will return with someone who would also assist. He returned with John McDonnell.

John had briefly met Ricky some years ago when he came to our door, canvassing to become a local MP in our borough. I was busy cooking dinner and left them talking. I remember Ricky asking John lots of questions. Later on he commented that John is "a nice and decent man who seems to care about his constituents".

Little did I know how true these words would become for Ricky himself.

John came into the sitting room with Suresh stating straight away that Suresh had updated him on the case, and he wanted to help us. Again, John has been one of the greatest advocates for Ricky's case and for justice, but also a friend and a supporter without whom we would not have got as far as we have.

At this point we all thought Ricky was just missing, maybe hurt somewhere and trying to find his way home. We decided to print posters, which we would paste all over Kingston and formed search groups to find Ricky. We thought it might trigger somebody's memory or they might have seen the racial attack that night.

Lots of people joined our search parties or carried out their own searches. Now that we were beginning to structure and organise ourselves rather than waiting for the police to decide whether they wanted to help, we were starting to make progress. On 18 October 1997, being Saturday, lots of my work colleagues, friends and family, a group of about 45 or 50 people distributed leaflets and appealed for witnesses all over Kingston. People were angry and did not understand why **the** police were not appealing for witnesses or searching for my son. Looking back, I do not remember seeing any police officers in Kingston during the first week. We also searched the parks and alleys in and around Kingston and also along the route of the bus Ricky would have caught, poking our sticks in the long grass to check whether Ricky was hurt and lying there. I have seen police do this when searching for missing people but they did not do this in Ricky's case.

I continued to telephone Uxbridge and Kingston police stations but received no response. It felt as if I were target practice in the centre of a field with Kingston and Uxbridge constabularies, taking turns to hit me with a ball that was shattering my heart, soul and body.

Uxbridge Police said the case is Kingston Police's responsibility as Ricky went missing there.

Kingston Police told me that the case is out of their jurisdiction because Ricky did not live there.

I was out of my depth and did not know what to do. Surely the police were there to help us—it was their job!? Not so. They only seemed interested in shifting responsibility without taking action to find out what had happened, meanwhile, allowing those first 24 hours, "the golden hours"—so crucial in any missing person's case—to dwindle away. The information lost in these golden hours is crucial. Everybody especially the police know how important these golden hours are to solve a crime. I kept on phoning the police stations to hear of any updates but did not receive any positive response. Towards the end of the day I was told by Uxbridge police station that Kingston were dealing with the case as the incident happened in Kingston. They told me more or less not to bother them. I phoned Kingston **and** I was told that as Ricky did not live in Kingston the investigation should be conducted by Uxbridge. When I said I was told by Uxbridge police that Kingston police were supposed to carry out the investigation, I was very curtly advised that the investigation had stopped due to lack of resources. I panicked. There had been missing persons' enquiries before, I had never heard of any cases where they had stopped police work due to lack of resources within 48 hours of someone going missing. So, why was there no money for Ricky's investigation. How and why was ths decision made within a few hours of Ricky going missing? Who authorised this action and on what basis? With a heavy heart, I realised I was being told that money was more important than Ricky's safety and life.

I was desperate and frightened and phoned John McDonnell. It was midnight and John told me that he would phone Kingston to clarify their position. He was told that the investigation would continue, and that it had never stopped, and they never told me that it had stopped! That was not true but they were evidently reluctant to show their disinterest to a Member of Parliament.

Both police stations refused to take ownership of the case. It appeared that the two were trying to "fob off" Ricky's disappearance to each other. Worried and confused, I thought nobody was interested in Ricky's case. They clearly assumed I would go away, sit quietly, and wait passively for answers. This issue was picked up in the then Police Complaints Authority Report and is included in John's copy in the Hansard which I talk about later in the book and the link to this article is also given.

When I asked what enquiries they had conducted, they could not give me a direct answer. By that time, I thought I had lost my mind. Surely, I wasn't the liar. I was distraught, grief stricken but could see that I was getting nowhere with the "so called investigation".

That night I collapsed. My family found me on the floor in Ricky's bedroom. My mind could not take any more of being lied to and gaslighted. I felt I was floating where nobody could see or hear me. I felt my son, his life was invisible to the people that had the power to help him.

Within days of Ricky going missing, I had a telephone call from *BBC News* telling me they wanted me to speak about Ricky's case. They sent a car to bring me to the studio. I had never visited a TV studio before and had no idea what to expect. In a daze I entered the studio, not knowing what I would need to do.

I was quickly ushered to the chair as we were running late. The host asked me to explain Ricky's case. She gave me a reassuring smile which calmed my nerves. I still don't know how I managed to do that interview. My first TV interview.

Days were spent on the streets in Kingston. Nights in Ricky's room. On his computer searching how to find missing persons. I was just a mum and was not trained to carry out these searches. I was in a state of panic—where do I start? What should I do? Who do I talk to? I had never been in this sort of situation before, but I had to learn. I had no choice.

Suresh accompanied me everywhere and offered my family practical and emotional support. Ricky's disappearance was widely publicised in the national press, on TV, radio, and more people started joining us and asking questions about the lack of police intervention. John kept in touch with us and helped with the communication with the police. By this time Ricky had been missing for a few days, less than a week.

I hardly slept and could not wait for the nights to end so that I could return to Kingston and start searching for my Ricky again. Kingston was pulling me towards something which at that time I did not understand. I just had a feeling that Ricky was somewhere in Kingston, hurt and unable to come home.

Mistakes, racial comments and lies from the police started from the first day and continued. I was frightened of my own thoughts, which were telling me that they were not interested in finding my son. We had to do it ourselves. I thought that any information I had gathered should be passed to the police to ensure it was checked or investigated by them. I clung to the hope they would actually do something to help.

As a young child, my parents told me and my siblings to contact the police if ever we were in trouble. They always believed police officers were honest and trustworthy as their job was to protect people and resolve crimes. We all believed our parents because surely they would not lie to us? I was following my parents' advice exactly, yet I was not being heard. I speak good English, I am educated, so surely they can understand me? If I was asking them to find my son, it was, and still is, my right. If not, where do I go?

There was not a single moment's peace from the relentless questions which plagued my mind day and night.

The role of a police officer is first to register and then to investigate crimes. To do so the officer needs to believe a crime has occurred. In this case, they knew about it within minutes. In order to carry out a proper investigation, there needs to be a belief in the status of the victim and an openness to explore the truth of what had really happened. The first police officer on the scene did not take any details and nor did the second one. Clearly they did not believe that a racial attack had taken place.

Assumptions made by Kingston Police reflected that in their eyes Black or Asian lives do not matter. They already implied Ricky had willingly run away from home because of stereotypical assumptions about how Indian families live their lives.

A few days later they searched our house. One police officer checked our garage with Balwant while the others checked inside of my house in my presence. I told them I had not harmed my son and was not hiding him in my house.

My children were distressed wanting to know why police were searching their home. My young son got frightened and hid behind his sister! I even told the police officer to use the ladder to search in my loft as I could not believe what was happening before my eyes. I felt like a criminal.

Mon got in touch with the Missing Persons Bureau, who sent some forms to us to complete and return. Another bureaucratic process with no immediate help.

People by then had heard about Ricky being missing and offered help. Suresh and John McDonnell played a big part and managed to assemble supporters who accompanied us in our search parties looking for Ricky in Kingston. Most of them wanted to know why we were searching for Ricky as it was a job for the police. They also said that they had seen no police officers searching for my son, no police officers had spoken to them when we were told they were carrying out enquiries.

Our family was always first to talk to people or to find witnesses. This was later confirmed during the inquest by people living in the boats close to where Ricky was found, and bus drivers or other people working and living in the area.

For the next seven days we continued to carry out our own enquiries. These included printing our own leaflets to hand out in Kingston and surrounding areas, talking to people on the roads, in cars, shops, wheelie bins, pubs, cab drivers, boat dwellers, building sites and late-night buses.

There were quite a few derelict buildings near the river at that time and because of the state of these buildings we formed human chains to enter these buildings in case Ricky was injured and lying there. I remember Balwant jumping in the big paladin and wheelie bins to see if someone had thrown Ricky in there.

We found CCTV cameras which we viewed and told police to seize them. Kingston police did not know about these cameras in their own town. Or if they did, they did not bother to collect them in time.

People supported us and assisted with distributing our leaflets, talking about the case to other people and trying to gather information in order to find Ricky. The momentum of this support from absolute strangers was both humbling and comforting whilst being an alien world to me.

My house during the first week was like a walk-in centre. Relatives and strangers came over to ask about Ricky, all offering support. Till this point, my family and I had lived a very undisturbed life. We had been in a sheltered sort of bubble, going to work, enjoying family life and had never had anything to do with police. Now, complete strangers offered support and later formed search parties armed with just torches but their hearts full of hope.

We printed and designed leaflets on our home PC computer. My children all slept in one room as they were too frightened and traumatised to sleep in their own rooms They were waiting for us, their parents, to return home with Ricky as I had promised. Hope in my children's eyes when I returned home tired and disappointed broke my heart but at the same time gave me courage to carry on with my searches. Every morning I was in a rush to leave home to go to Kingston to search for Ricky but reluctant to return home empty handed. My children were always rushing to open the door to see if Ricky was with us and then disappointed, returned to their rooms I could see their pain and frustration clearly in their eyes but was unable to do anything and sometimes had no words to console them. I felt all empty.

Ricky (left of image) caught on CCTV near Wood Street moments after the racist attack

We had located some CCTV cameras within two days and were shown the footage where Dean recognised himself. We also located another camera where Ricky is seen walking by, near the corner of the town centre.

We located further cameras and informed the police. I was angry they had not bothered to look for these cameras as these would have helped them in their investigation.

One of the cameras we located and viewed which was later handed to the police showed a fleeting glimpse of my son, at 21 minutes past midnight, which I believe was the last time Ricky was seen by anyone except his killers. It was the last time I saw him alive on the camera as well.

My gut sense was that the police thought there was no need for a proper investigation as the missing person was only an Asian! Their comments and inaction had already told me they were not at all concerned about the racial attack. In fact, they rarely referred to it. When we raised it, they tried to shift the conversation away to other subjects.

Whenever we located CCTV cameras we were told we would not have access to these cameras due to the Data Protection Act, only the police were allowed to collect them, so we informed the police. In some instances, the police were too late and the tapes were either destroyed or wiped. There are cameras everywhere in Kingston and I was shocked to learn the police seemed unaware of their existence or didn't seem bothered as this would involve real work. which in my opinion they thought was not necessary? They did not believe that an Asian woman would question their investigation. Not a lot of Sikh women at that time challenged the authorities but my love for my son made me stand up and do so.

I did press and public appeals for information which included appearing on TV, offering a substantial reward. I even arranged for our own reconstruction on TV. Mr Tommy Nagra, a friend and supporter arranged this. My mind was in a state of frenzy wanting to know why no proper investigation was being done when in other similar cases police had moved heaven and earth to do so!

It was clear as day that Ricky had been attacked and immediately following the attack, had disappeared. How much louder did the alarm bells need to ring for the police to take his disappearance seriously?

I would leave our children at home in the mornings to go to Kingston to search for Ricky. Balwant and Mon always accompanied me. Suresh joined us as without him we would not have coped or known what to do. He helped coordinate searches.

I kept in contact with my children over the telephone. They were carrying out their own investigations by ringing bus and cab drivers etc., to see if they had seen anything connected to Ricky that night. They located the route of buses that left Bentalls Shopping Centre towards Uxbridge that night.

I was using Ricky's phone because I did not own one. They

were still very much a novelty at that time. Using Ricky's phone meant he was with me. I knew my children needed me, but while my whole body was on fire, finding their missing brother was all I thought about. They stayed at home, helping, and hoping. Ricky's disappearance was widely circulated by the

The leaflet distrbuted by family and friends during the week that Ricky was missing

huge media interest. They could not cope with other children asking questions about Ricky at school or at university.

It was also accompanied by another story widely circulated by the press... a young man had been kidnapped in London.

Ricky did not have his mobile phone, and I could not contact him. If he was not on the ground, had his attackers thrown him in the river? I could not shake this fear.

I asked the police to search the river and was told it had already been done. This reassured me in some ways but alarmed me in others... if he was not in the water, then he must be lying somewhere badly injured or kept somewhere against his will—that was also my fear which I was unable to shake off.

With intensifying anguish, we continued with our searches. I fell over frequently but did not care. Whatever food was put before me I would eat, but nourishment was not on my mind. Was Ricky hungry? Adrenaline brought me back from the frailty of exhaustion each time. A few days later, Detective Inspector Morgan came to tell us he had been appointed as "consultant". I did not understand what that meant nor what his role in the investigation was. He went away the next day and said, for a few days, somebody else would look at the case.

Ms Little, a Family Liaison Office, was appointed to keep us updated about any developments. She should have been informing us of actions planned or undertaken by the police, and—one would think—to support the family, but most of the time Ms Little had no news. When questioned by us she said she would "find out" and "inform us the next day". It felt like she was there more to get information out of us than anything else. The hindsight provided by what we now know about the Spy Cops scandal only reinforces that view."

People kept saying how brave I was to do what I was doing. I was not doing it alone. I had lots of friends, supporters and family members helping me to find Ricky. It was the most agonising time for all involved. Bravery on its own was not enough. I had hope as well as fear. Ricky would come back—harmed or injured—but he would come back.

Fear that something might prevent me from doing these tasks propelled me and kept me busy from the time I woke to the time I would go to sleep, for a moment, until reality crashed into comfort.

I would never be allowed to sleep peacefully while Ricky was missing. I am still not permitted or granted this privilege.

The police decided to put an appeal out for information about Ricky's disappearance on the seventh day. A press conference was scheduled at SMG. I was due to speak and went to Southall, leaving my children at home.

Upon arrival at the SMG offices late morning 21 October 1997, Suresh had a phone call from the police who advised him to keep me in his office as they had some news about Ricky.

At the same time, I received a telephone call from my daughter asking me if she should open the door to Ms Little. I told her she could.

I had instructed my children to keep the door closed when I was not at home. People were coming over to ask about Ricky and how they could assist us. Obviously people were interested and helpful, but my children were already traumatised. I did not want anyone upsetting them more by asking questions about their brother. I had to leave them alone at home but at the same time protect them in any way I thought was possible.

While I was waiting for the police to arrive, I telephoned my daughter again. She told me that two police officers were in my house. Then suddenly our call got disconnected. I thought perhaps she had accidentally terminated my call... I called her back but no one answered... I rang again... the telephone was dead.

Suresh tried to telephone, but there was no response. While I was trying to understand the problem with the phone at home, the police officer came to the Southall Monitoring Group with the news that Ricky was dead and unbeknown to my children, not only their brother was dead but their mother also died on that day.

Chapter 2

A Son and a Brother

A joyous day on 11 July 1977
A son and a brother placed in my arms
Some cruel people ended his life
On 14 October 1997, by whom and why was he harmed?

I was born in Nairobi, East Africa to a Punjabi Sikh family. My parents migrated to Kenya from India in the 1940s and settled there. My father, Mr Amar Singh Matharu, was working as a Supervisor Centre Lathe Operator. He enjoyed his job and worked six days a week. My father worked hard and made sure we all went to good schools. Education was very important to him and he wanted us to stand on our own feet and become independent. He was very young when his own father died and so being the eldest all the family's responsibility fell on him and I think that made him more determined that none of us would rely on others, if we wanted anything we had to work for it.

My mother, Mrs Gurdial Kaur Matharu, was a stay-at-home-mum. She was there for us all the time. She made sure we all had a full breakfast before leaving home, our clothes were always washed and ironed. Fresh food was prepared every day. She was always ready to greet us with a big smile on our return to home after school. She mended our clothes, stayed up all night when we were ill. She was our Home Minister, the one who everybody needed and relied on.

I had three sisters and two brothers. Our childhood was good and comfortable and my parents fulfilled most of our wishes within their means. My parents were kind, honest and humble people. They had a beautiful and supportive relationship.

Nairobi was a beautiful country. It was rich in different kinds of fruit and I always remember big juicy mangoes. The population consisted of people from all over the world and most of my childhood is surrounded by good memories. We never questioned anybody's colour or religion. We studied, worked and socialised with people from all backgrounds, faiths and religions.

My father was provided with a truck and a driver by his employer. The driver used to drop him home and leave the truck in front of our house. He would return in the morning to take my dad back to work together with other employees. We loved that truck and all the children around our house would climb in that truck and play games. It was a simple but fulfilling life, and it was what we made of it.

My mother's family lived in Uganda in East Africa. We visited them on the train when we could. My father's family lived in India except for one sister who lived near us. We had a big extended family and visited each other quite often. There was never a shortage of family, and therefore of fun, laughter and companionship.

Mon had a dog called Tiger. Sometimes all of us would go out for a walk in the evening and he always accompanied us. One day somebody threw something on him which resulted in boils on his skin. My mother washed Tiger with antibiotics until he got well. My neighbours thought that this was strange but my mother treated Tiger like he was her child. She had nothing but love, and taught us the same.

My parents were always ready to help other people whenever they could. I remember when one of the neighbour's daughters was getting married. The chef advised he had run out of flour to make chapattis for lots of guests. My dad quietly went to the shop and ordered and paid for a big bag of flour and had it delivered to the neighbours' house stating that the driver of the shop had forgotten to deliver it. He did that so the guests of the bride's mother would not know that she had no money to buy more flour.

This was our upbringing and we all learned to be patient, self-sufficient, feel and share other people's pain and be helpful to other people in need. This is what I also passed on to my children. I am proud that my children have continued with my teachings. Doing something positive for someone is like winning the lottery.

After finishing my studies at Khalsa Primary School in Nairobi I went to the Duchess of Gloucester Secondary School. There was no free schooling or NHS in Nairobi. My father always paid all his bills on time. His motto was "live within your means" and don't expect anything from anyone. We finally understood what he was trying to teach us when we became adults. We went to school with children of different faiths and religions but everyone got on with each other. I first heard the word "racism" mentioned when I came to England. It never occurred to us that we were any different from other people. My parents never taught us that. Everyone was welcome to our house.

There was political unrest in Kenya at the time and people were scared in case things got out of hand. Lots of burglaries and murders were taking place and my father sent my mother and all his children to India until things calmed down.

We sailed by ship to India in 1965. This was the mode of travel in those days. We were all young and did not understand my parents' worries, but sailing by ship was a big adventure and I really enjoyed it. I believe we were at sea for 11-12 days and every moment was a pure joy. I used to go to the deck after dinner and sit there for hours watching the sea and stars. Sometimes I wrote poetry sitting under the stars and listened to huge waves. I did not have a care in the world. I loved life. On arrival in India my mother rented a flat in Ludhiana in Punjab. I met my father's family in India for the first time, especially my grandmother. I saw her quite often and wanted her to live with us. She refused because she had lived independently all her life since my grandfather had died. She brought her four children up by herself without asking for any help from anyone.

I went to school there and passed my exams with good grades. In the holidays I learned to type and do shorthand and became good at it. It came in handy when I started my employment later in the UK. We returned to Kenya in 1966 and after a few months I came to England to join Mon.

Mon was already here. My parents thought I should live with my grandparents in Leeds as I had never lived on my own. I felt lonely in Leeds so after two months I decided to join Mon in London. It was difficult to find an office job for an Asian girl in those days in Leeds. I started working in a shirt factory but managed to secure a clerical job after a few weeks.

I studied in my spare time and attended several training courses. I managed to get a job as a secretary in London in a well-known Marine company. I married Balwant in 1975 and both of us worked really hard and managed to buy a small house. Our first child was a daughter. She brought a lot of joy to our family and still does.

Balwant was obsessed with her as he had always wanted a little girl to dote on. Every time we went out he was the one wanting to push the pram. He would come home with something for her all the time. I returned to work and placed my daughter with a child minder whose children had grown up and she loved my girl like her own. Later on my parents joined us for a while and looked after my daughter.

Then on 11 July 1977 Ricky was born. I felt the whole world was happy when Ricky was placed into my arms A baby who was staring straight at me and smiling. He was holding my finger tightly. He trusted me to look after him and I hugged him and felt that I was the luckiest mother. He was quite a large baby weighing six pounds.

I felt I was walking on air and I remember the nurse telling me off for running downstairs six hours after giving birth. From a baby I watched Ricky grow into a toddler. We named him Lakhvinder, which means "loved by many". Ricky was his nickname. Little did I realise at the time that millions of people will know and love Ricky tragically after his death.

He was a happy and content baby. I proudly brought him home a few days after birth. His favourite toys were cars, superman and watching cartoons on TV like Tom and Jerry when he was a baby. He had an older sister to play with who loved him and our life was complete. They were close in age so grew up together.

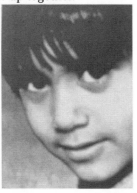 

I wanted to be a full-time mother and resigned from my employment. My parents moved into their own property. They adored my children and the children loved them.

Ricky was always the quiet one. The sparkle in his eyes and the cheeky grin always made me aware when he was thinking of any mischief, especially when he played with his siblings.

On the way to his first day at playgroup, Ricky was quite happy but when I tried to leave him he started crying. The group leader asked me to leave as she wanted to settle him down. Later she told me he had stopped crying as soon as I left. I was more upset at leaving him there. When he returned he put his arms around me and told me he did not want to be away from me. On the first day at school nursery I introduced him as Lakhvinder to his teacher but he told her he wanted to be known as Ricky.

I could not forget Balwant's laughter when I put a bowl on Ricky's head and cut his hair making sure the length was ok. I did this as Ricky refused to go to the hairdresser the first time. He thought she would cut his ear! I never dared to do that again and always took Ricky to the hairdressers.

He loved everything about school. He always checked his school bag to make sure his books were there and his homework was done on time. I spent the evenings with my children to help them with their homework and other activities. He loved his cookery class and once made a pizza which I refused to eat as I thought it contained meat. But unknown to me he had specially made a vegetarian one for me. He was really happy when I ate it. He said it was a surprise for me.

Ricky with his baby brother

My second daughter was born three years after Ricky. My children were thrilled when I had my last baby, which happened to be a boy, especially Ricky as he wanted a boy to play football with him. One day when I went to check my sleeping baby I found Ricky with a rolled up tissue trying to poke it up the tip of the baby's nose. He said he wanted the baby to get up so he could play with him. Ricky was shy but affectionate. (photo 3)

All the children after finishing their schools went to universities. The Headmaster of the primary school describes Ricky as "*a quiet rather serious boy of above average ability and is well remembered for his polite manner and his consideration to others. His behaviour was exemplary and I remember no occasion when he was in trouble of any kind".* Ricky did well at school. He believed in hard work and developed a love of computers at a time when they were rare.

Ricky chose to work as a porter in a hospital for a week during his school work experience. His friends chose to work in offices, shops, but he wanted to help people. He said this helped him to understand how vulnerable we all are and how life could change in a minute.

Ricky passed his GCSE examinations with good marks and enrolled at Langley Grammar School, in the sixth form, to undertake two years of A level study between 1993 to 1995. He studied Computer Science, Sociology and Economics.

Mrs Boyd, his tutor, describes Ricky as:

> *always a co-operative student with a quiet, reliable personality. The staff found him very dependable and he supported them by helping voluntarily with junior pupils in the computer room during lunch times. Assignments in his A level subjects were always completed on time and he had a mature sense of time management. He was determined to succeed. Lakhvinder was a popular student, well integrated into the group. He had a quiet*

sense of humour and was always punctual, polite and utterly dependable.

He took part in various drama productions, including one production where their group went to junior schools to show a piece of work they had done about Responsibility in and out of the home. He was also a school Prefect and enjoyed playing badminton, hockey, squash, tennis and swimming. Even though Ricky loved swimming and was very good at it, he had a phobia of open water, a fact which would become crucial later on.

Ricky's school photograph

Ricky passed his A level examination with good grades. His first choice was to study at Brunel University but was offered Loughborough University, a good two-hour trip from home. After about two weeks he telephoned and said he did not like living away from home and wanted to move to Brunel University, which was 10 minutes down the road. He arranged the transfer himself and started at Brunel University in 1995 and was studying Computer Science and Management Science. The tutors thought very highly of him. Ricky wanted to graduate and start his own business. Mr Robert Ayres, his tutor at Brunel University, describes Ricky as *"a polite, cheerful and very pleasant young man who had a keen interest in computers and took his studies seriously. On the basis of his second year results I would have expected him to graduate with a good degree. I have no doubt that he would have been very successful in his chosen career after university"*.

During his first year at Brunel he stayed in student halls. He came home at weekends saying he missed the family and I laughed saying he missed my cooking. In the first week he brought a bag of washing and wanted to know why his white towel had turned blue, which he had washed at the university. He had put a mixed wash of colours and white clothes in the washing machine. The dye from his jeans had changed the colour of his towel. I could not stop laughing but he wanted to know why the colour changed. After that incident he would always bring clothes home to wash but did eventually learn to do his own washing properly. He had friends from school and made more at university. He did not go out much. He spent his spare time on his computer creating educational programs which he tested on his younger brother. He also spent some time at his general practitioner's surgery learning about different computer programs which they had installed at that time.

He returned home after completing the first year. He got a car and drove to his university or sometimes used public transport. Meanwhile my eldest daughter was living away at university.

Ricky successfully completed two years at Brunel and was undergoing a work placement for a year at Open Mind Design in Central London in August 1997. He was working and was also being encouraged to study and thus successfully completed Microsoft SQL Server, a comprehensive Hands-On Introduction course, on 26 September 1997. Mr Smith, his employer at Open Mind Design, says

> *Ricky impressed us immediately. Very smart and dapper with a cheery smile, he exuded confidence, but confidence without any sort of arrogance we had seen from one or two of the earlier candidates.*
>
> *Quiet confidence is hard to find in staff but Ricky had it in abundance.*

He always showed excellent concentration with his work and never took a single day off due to sickness. He had a clear idea of what he wanted to do with his future.

In person he was very shy unless directly asked a question, where he'd be chatty and friendly.

I was very impressed with the way he seemed to learn complex things very quickly. All the clients who met him liked him—but then you couldn't not like him.

At work if he hit a problem he would work away at it until he solved it instead of asking for help, which is unusual for someone so young and in first year of the job.

He worked hard, often in complete silence, and got to grips with some very difficult technologies amazingly quickly. It was only after his death that I found his briefcase, which revealed course notes and exercises showing that he had also been working quite hard on things on his own PC at home 'out of hours'.

He never at any time appeared depressed or low. On the day of his disappearance, he was given permission to leave early as he had a conference that he was due to attend the next day as he had an early start. He was really looking forward to the day and appeared cheerful and relaxed.

The thing we all miss most about Ricky is his smile and laughter. His whole face would light up when he smiled and he had very mischievous eyes that shouted 'fun' at you. He seemed to be someone who was more than happy with life, and he seemed to take genuine pride and enjoyment at work.

Personally I always think of Ricky as an 'impeccable

Englishman'. This may seem odd given his Asian heritage, but for me his voice (*with an "educated" English accent) and general demeanour epitomised what I think of as the best of the qualities of the 'old world' Englishman— qualities of politeness, diligence and charm.

Most of Ricky's spare time was spent on computers. One day I went to Ricky's room to find him on the computer with his new programme about Maths which he was testing on his brother, who was looking at me with pleading eyes to rescue him because he wanted to go to the garden and play! At weekends he would take his sisters to a library or just help his dad with refurbishment of our house. He was relaxed, content and focused.

I recall a time when my husband and Ricky were digging the garden and took a break. I thought I would go and help so I started digging. Ricky came over straight away and took the axe from my hands and told me that it was not a job for me and started digging. Later I found him sitting in the kitchen with a towel on his hands. His hands were covered with blisters. When he saw tears in my eyes he quickly hid his hands and told me laughingly to go and look at his dad's hands. He was very shy and did not want any fuss but with his siblings he would spend a whole night talking about studies, films, music and politics. He was very close to his two sisters.

Ricky was extremely calm and collected. He was very motivated and determined to get the best out of life and be successful, not only in the business world but also in life in general. Ricky achieved much in his short life due to his focused and mature attitude. He avoided getting distracted by menial matters and therefore was able to get on with life and achieve whilst others simply watched or thought. Ricky's outlook on life was quite mature and he was never fearful of any obstacles which came in his way. If he ever encountered any problems he always found ways to overcome them.

Our family was like any other working-class family. We worked hard to build a future for our children. Balwant was a carpenter and almost worked seven days a week. He renovated our house when he did not work on weekends. When the children were very young, we decided we would look after them ourselves.

Balwant worked during the day and came home between 5.30 and 6 pm, when I would be waiting near the door to rush out to start my job at 6 pm and return home at 1.30 am. Later on as the children became older I started working full time when my youngest son turned five. I was promoted at work, which would mean working for longer hours. When I mentioned this to my family, Ricky reassured me and told me not to worry as everyone would look after each other and share chores to help me with housework! And he kept his word. Even my youngest child started to put his plates in the dishwasher!

Ricky and his dad together worked on lots of projects around the house. They were more like friends. My children used to gather in a room and have discussions on different topics. I used to laugh that all of them were putting this world right. Everybody had a different view which would end with laughter or an argument. Ricky said that the girls always got the majority as their brother was too young to join in their discussions/debates. Ricky had a unique sense of humour and I could tell as his eyes used to sparkle with mischief. There were trips to the supermarket in Ricky's car and also trips to the hospital where he stayed with me for hours refusing to leave my side even though he had examinations the next day. When I tried to force him to leave he just hugged me and said he could always take his exams later but he could not get another mother like me! I knew that he was cheering me up as I was quite ill.

There was always laughter in the house, which I now miss. Sometimes I think I have forgotten how to laugh. My eldest daughter said

> *I am Ricky's older sister. There was only 18 months between us. Not much really but we were so different. Ricky was a quiet person whereas I was the opposite. I think I made a noise for both of us! I also have a younger*

sister and a younger brother. My sister is around five years younger than me and my brother 10 years.

Ricky and I both went to a Primary together, then we both went to the same secondary school. I always remember walking with him, but he would always walk ahead of me and I would always be behind him. A typical brother from what I remember! At school we had our own sets of friends and kept a look out for each other.

During the holidays, my mum and dad were working so we would spend our summers in either Leamington Spa or we would go and stay at my grandma's house. They are very fond memories that I hold dear to me and I remember feeling carefree and happy.

As like most teenagers we were both very keen to learn how to drive. Ricky passed his test the first time, but I passed the third time! I remember my parents bought us both an old blue VW polo. It was a difficult car to drive, as it had a manual choke. The first and second gear were next to each other, so when we pulled off at the traffic lights, we would either go forward or backwards! We had a car, so we couldn't complain. As usual Ricky would usually call shotgun so I rarely drove when we were together. He was a safe and reliable driver, that was our Ricky, always erring on the side of caution.

GCSEs came and went for the both of us. Ricky was a talented student. He always spent time 'messing' with computers in his room. He rarely left it to be honest as it was his hobby.

Dinner times were like most families, hectic and noisy. Mum always made a fuss at dinner time, and always made home cooked food. Takeaways were a rarity in our house as mum and dad both cooked everything.

Most days of the week we ate Indian cuisine and we had to eat up all our meals before we left the table. I remember one time my mum took the tablecloth off and found some chapatis (Indian flatbread) under the tablecloth. We found out that Ricky had stuffed it under the table! We all laughed about this as Ricky was the most unlikely candidate to have done this!

Once we had both finished school and got our university place, we both left home to study. Ricky started at Loughborough University. He only lasted a week then felt homesick. He ended up going to Brunel University, only a few minutes from our home. I went to study at Northampton so after that we only saw each other at weekends. Ricky had got a job at this time at our local Currys, so we saw each other even less.

If I had known how precious time was going to be, I would have taken more trips home to spend time with him. Something I will always regret.   •

I was in my second year at University when I received a phone call from my mum to say my little brother was missing. I remember thinking this was out of character for my brother as he rarely went out to socialise. I knew then that something was wrong that night, because I remember crying uncontrollably as I felt I was never going to see him again. That is the night I think I really grieved.

The next day my housemate drove me home, so I could be home with my family. At this stage I was very anxious as I hadn't had any updates from my family of Ricky's disappearance so was dreading pulling up at home to see what I was coming home to.

I remember my little sister being very upset that night. We slept in the same room that night and she held my hand most of the night. The next few days with the help of family and friends we searched strategically, posters were made up and search parties were organised. I remember one evening I just stopped and thought, when was the last time I combed my hair? I couldn't get a hairbrush through it and I couldn't understand why. A very random thought that I have never forgotten. Those days were a blur, I don't remember eating or sleeping, just lots of people in our house and lots of noise.

When the news was broken to us kids about Ricky's death I remember not registering and just carried on. It was like I was in a film and was being watched so I had to carry on acting. I remember looking at my mum and dad and seeing my mum break down uncontrollably and my dad just numb standing there. It was all happening in slow motion. A few days later it was all public knowledge and I didn't feel in control anymore, our lives were like an open book.

The days up to the funeral I remember were so busy. I went regularly to the funeral parlour with my mum just so I could see Ricky. I guess I felt guilty as before I left to go back to university one weekend, I remember having an argument with Ricky over something very trivial as I was leaving and he was on the stairs. I felt I had to see him to apologise. I made the most of those visits with my parents just to see him and be near him.

I went to the morgue with my mum as many times as I could just to be close to him. I remember looking at his cold body and trying to touch it to see if that was really my brother. But all I could feel was the coarse stitches on his cold skin. I needed to feel it to make myself feel that this is real and I didn't need to pinch myself, I just needed to touch his cold hands.

I wore a green suit to the funeral, one I knew Ricky would like, I didn't want to wear white as that was the tradition. I wanted to celebrate his life! I had my arm across the coffin when it was on display as I wanted to protect him from the prying eyes. He didn't look like Ricky any more, but to everyone else he did, so I had to stand guard to make sure he was going to be okay, that was the least I could do for my little brother as this was the last time I was going to see him.

I live with this now and have learnt to make time for my siblings as this relationship is so precious.

I have three children. A boy and two girls. I make sure every day that they know how lucky they are to have each other and appreciate each other as you don't know how short life can be.

As Ricky's big sister I have a lot of fond memories of my brother. We used to play many imaginary games when we were young. One particular happy memory I have was when we all used to go to my grandma's house. We used to all rush upstairs and jump on my Uncle's bed and pretend we were on a ship! We would imagine that the sea was surrounding us and the waves were crashing on the side of the boat! In the rough sea there were sharks trying to eat us! What an imagination we had when we were young. I am sure Ricky also had an imaginary friend!

Another fond memory is of going to Littlehampton in the summer with my mum and dad. My mum used to make all the food and pack a bag for the beach. My dad would be the designated driver. We all used to get so excited when we would see the signs for the beach. My mum would be in charge of the food and bags at the beach and my dad would hold our hands and take us into the water to have a splash around. Ricky would always hesitate but with my dad holding his hand would only just dip his feet in the water. I remember seeing his happy smiley face near the water with his 'bowler' haircut and his shrieks of laughter. They were good times that I will cherish. I have even taken my kids there to help me remember and share the memories with them.

Memories are all I have left now and what I hold onto. I will never forget Ricky and don't want to forget him so the memories are even more precious. They live on through my children, when I tell them stories and show them pictures of their uncle.

My son has some of the same characteristics as Ricky, he is also the quiet, shy and the sensible type. They have similar eyes as well. His twin sister always asks questions about him. "What was he like mummy?". "You must still miss him mummy?" She is inquisitive and likes to hear stories about her uncle she has never seen.

My eldest daughter has supported my mum and me when we have had low points. She is someone I can rely on to listen and support me. She was the first grandchild in our family and Ricky would have doted on her.

When I graduated, got married and had my children, I always thought to myself, Ricky would be so proud of me. He would have made a great brother-in-law, and uncle."

My younger daughter wrote "I am Ricky's younger sister. By three years. I am now 41 years old. Ricky was 20 years old when he died. I am now two decades older than he was. This is my story of Ricky and who he was to me and what his death meant to me...

I have a younger brother too, who is six years younger than me and an older sister who was just a year older than Ricky. There were four of us. And now there are three.

As a sibling group my two brothers, my sister and I were always close. I have happy memories of all of them. We thought we would always have each other.

Ricky was really different to me though and perhaps that's why we were so close. He was quiet when I was loud as a child, he was more shy where I was more confident. He was quite a homebody when I was much more outgoing. He liked to sit at home and spend hours on his computer, writing programs and reading up about coding. He had a very practical mind. I was more interested in going out with my friends, hanging out after school and being popular. He was interested in looking after our parents, getting a good job, he was focused. I was more interested in having fun.

I suppose he was the sensible one out of the four of us, reliable, grounded and very serious. He was focused on what he wanted out of life, which was a career in IT at a time when we were still using dial-up modems and the world of IT was an emerging, exciting prospect. I still remember him getting annoyed if anyone used the phone when he was trying to connect to the internet using the agonisingly slow dial up connection.

Ricky was shy. It's something everyone who knew him remembers about him. He was shy, even at home. My other siblings and I were probably quite loud and rowdy by comparison. That didn't stop him joining in with our games. When my younger brother, nine years Ricky's junior, was a toddler, the three of us used to build forts for our baby brother in the living room and chase my little brother through the nooks and crannies and tunnels that we built using the sofa and the living room curtains draped over the top. They were fun times. Everything was simple. We enjoyed each other's company. We had parents who loved us. We had everything we needed. We had known no hardships.

Ricky was shy, yes, but he also had a rather coy sense of humour. It was one of his finest qualities because it meant that when he did laugh, when he did crack a joke, he was so happy, it made you happy. His smile was infectious, it was huge and his eyes when he laughed had such a sparkle to them.

I remember Ricky used to go in at night to my little brother's room when he was asleep in his little toddler bed and tease him before bedtime. In very short order that would lead to my mum running up the stairs telling Ricky off and to tell him to stop annoying his little brother at bedtime. Ricky would find this hilarious and scarper back to his bedroom before my mum could get up the stairs.

Which made him laugh even more. And when Ricky laughed, you couldn't help but laugh because it was nice to see someone who was so 'sensible' find the fun in a special moment.

I recollect once our little brother broke his tiny baby toe. Ricky would take him to and from school, and really looked after him. My dad told my little brother to soak his foot in a bowl of warm water with turmeric, an old Indian remedy that my father had been taught by his parents. Of course, this turned my brother's entire foot a fairly bright shade of yellow, which we all found hilarious but Ricky in particular teased my little brother endlessly about his 'yellow foot' for days afterwards.

Another memory I have is when Ricky was teasing my little brother and my little brother pushed him in retaliation. Ricky was nine years older and my younger brother was tiny yet Ricky ended up landing a spread eagle on top of the coffee table, which at that time had wheels on which was all the rage in the early 90s. The table continued to travel down the length of the kitchen with Ricky on it crashing into the wall at the far end. Ricky was so shocked that my little brother had pushed him. After he got over the initial shock, he thought it was hilarious and could not stop laughing, much to my mother's chagrin. Both were promptly ticked off and sent off to their bedrooms

On Sunday mornings my dad would make a 'fry up' breakfast for all of us along with my mum. It was a ritual, every Sunday morning. Ricky had a habit where he had to eat his breakfast leaving one mouthful of each item on his breakfast plate so he could have one perfect mouthful of every item at the end to finish off his breakfast. We used to tease him about it. He said it was a perfect way to finish off his breakfast.

Even evening meals could also be quite humorous. Whilst our parents weren't looking, Ricky would do funny things at the dinner to make us laugh, subtly though so as not to draw the attention of our parents. He'd empty our glasses of water back into the pitcher on the table leaving us confused as to where it had gone when we went to take a sip. He'd move our cutlery around or hide it. He had a great, unique sense of humour. It wasn't the type of humour where he'd laugh out loud all the time. It was a quiet, cheeky sense of humour that we all enjoyed. I miss it, even now. Life seems a lot duller for the loss of his special sense of humour.

I was really close to Ricky. I suppose it was because I was a tomboy growing up. We'd go out riding our bikes together, and I was one of the privileged few who was allowed to play on this computer, which was his favourite thing in the whole world.

We also (and I'm not sure he would thank me for sharing the story) set up a little library in a small storage cupboard in our house, upstairs next to mine and my sister's bedroom. We emptied the shelves and put all our books on there and made library cards and we would take turns being librarians and borrowing books. It probably wasn't the coolest pastime but it was the 90s and there wasn't much else to do!

Ricky was really close to my dad as well. During his teens my dad was undertaking a mammoth extension on our house. He would lift the breeze blocks, help mix the cement, he helped with painting and varnishing, which was the obligatory mahogany 1990's colour of choice. He wanted to learn all the skills that my dad had. He was genuinely interested and valued them. He never complained or moaned that he had better things to do. Even now, when we have had to make improvements or repairs to the house, I can see it's really hard for my dad to paint over the paint that Ricky painted, or to change the mahogany varnish because he painted that on. There are little memories and echoes of Ricky all throughout the house, reverberations of him. At times my parents have been approached to sell the house but they've just been unable to part with it because it's where Ricky lived and it's where he used his own hands to build or paint and decorate parts of the house.

One great memory I've got of Ricky is of long ago when skinny jeans first came into fashion during the late 80s and early 90s. He asked my mum to tighten his jeans using her sewing machine as she was and still is a dab hand at all things seamstress. She promptly tightened his jeans and he put them on, but they had been tightened so much that he couldn't get them off again and it took three of us to yank them off. It's a story I still tell my children, about their uncle and 'his skinny jeans' which they find hilarious. It's a fond memory, because it's of him laughing, and then us laughing together. I loved it when he laughed.

These are just some of my memories of my big brother. I loved him so much that it hurts to think about him. I'm happy when I remember these moments, flashes of history, of times never to return, but also so hurt, that I'll never see that coy smile and those twinkling big brown eyes again.

In those last few years before he died Ricky had started to come out of his shell. I remember I was badgering him

all the time telling him to get himself out there, to go out with his friends, now that he was in university. I was probably living vicariously through him telling him to do all the things that as a young sister I wasn't allowed to do yet. I teased him about what he wore, telling him where to shop for clothes and what to buy.

When he started at Brunel University things changed a little. He was having a fantastic time, working in the IT industry whilst doing his degree in Computer

Science. The University was 10 minutes down the road from where we lived. He had been awarded a place at Loughborough University where he attended for a week living in student halls but returned home after a week saying he wanted to live at home, which he did, from his second year onwards when he transferred to Brunel. He got a weekend Job at Currys electrical stores selling technology, and loved it. With his first wage, he chose to spend it on buying the family our first big screen TV. He made friends at university who were a bit more outgoing than he was and the night of 14 October 1997, the day he died, was the first proper time he had really gone out.

The last picture we ever took of him was on 1 February 1997, my parents' anniversary. Back then we used cameras with film that needed to be taken to a shop and developed! We were going out to an Indian restaurant and he came downstairs in his new leather jacket and his new purple Adidas sweatshirt looking fashionable! He was wearing his new fly button jeans with his black buckle shoes. He had his famous silky black hair freshly cut into a 'step' haircut shaved at the sides long at the top. At the bottom of the staircase as he descended, I told him to stop as I had my camera out and I took a picture

of him. He smiled into the camera. I was frankly shocked he agreed to pose for a picture at all! Sadly, it would be the picture that would end up on his Missing Persons Poster. I have kept that sweatshirt and still wear it. My children call it the 'Ricky Reel Jumper'.

Later that year in 1997 he started his Placement in Industry as part of his degree and he began this with a small but lovely firm, and he absolutely loved it despite the commute into London every day. My mum would drop him at Hounslow train station on her own way into work. You could see that he absolutely loved what he was doing. Even his work bag was immaculately arranged with his folder and his pencil case. After he died, I took that pencil case and I still have the stationery that he used. Including the blue IBM pencil and the blue and silver Parker pen. It was his, and now it is mine.

On the last night I saw him on 14 October 1997 everything was normal. It was my little brother's parents' evening at his grammar school that night and I was going with my mum. Ricky was going out that night. I think it was only the first or second time he had gone out to a nightclub. There was a gig at the student union at Brunel University and he was going with some of his university friends. My mum and I went out to go to the parents' evening at about 7 o'clock that evening and at that time Ricky was still at home and I remember being super excited for him, as he was going out, and I remember he asked me about what he should wear before I left. He told my mum he'd be home by 1 o'clock in the morning. I had no idea that evening that it would be the last time I would ever see him. I wish I'd known. I'd have never let him go.

The next morning, the house was already alive with activity. My mum was on the phone and Ricky wasn't home. She was calling around to the police and trying to find out who Ricky's friends were. Ricky had barely gone out before, let alone never come home. This was totally unprecedented. Immediately we knew something wasn't right. I thought he'd walk in the door late that morning, tell us his battery on his mobile phone had died and everything would be okay. Never did it cross my mind that he was dead. As it turns out he must already have been dead for several hours. It haunts me even now, knowing that when I was walking round, going to school, he was cold, dead, lifeless, in the lonely icy waters of the Thames, gone forever.

Ricky had those huge brick-like mobile phones at a time when hardly anyone had a mobile phone and after his death, my mum took over his contract and the number that she uses is actually his telephone number.

We tried ringing it over and again, but there was no answer. My mum told me to go to school, not to worry, that they would find Ricky and so I went to school. She told me not to worry but the worry was there in her eyes. I had just started sixth form, in Year 12. At lunch break, I went out and I found a payphone. I rang home and my mum told me that they still hadn't been able to get hold of Ricky and at that point I really started to panic and worry. I got a lift home with a friend from school and as we pulled into my road, I could see my uncle's car was parked outside the house and I knew something was very wrong and clearly Ricky wasn't home.

That next week my sister and I spent every hour that we could on the phone. My sister had been at university at the time and she came home. Between us we looked after our younger brother, who was only 11 at the time and had just started grammar school. We rang taxi firms, hospitals, nightclubs and we kept a running list. Each phone call began with hope, each one ended with disappointment.

My parents were out trawling the streets of Kingston all day, every day, including at one or two o'clock in the morning, trying to jog the memory of anyone who would've been out at the same time that Ricky was in Kingston that night. All of my family came to our home to help, our cousins, aunties and uncles, helping with searching and making enquiries and I will eternally be grateful to them. We produced leaflets on Ricky's computer to try and find Ricky. Not for a moment did it cross my mind that Ricky wouldn't come home. I thought he was injured or hurt or being held against his will. Things like this didn't happen to families like us or so I thought at the time. Ricky's friends during that week were frequent visitors to the home.

I remember thinking how badly Ricky was going to be told off when he came home by my parents. Still thinking he would come home. Young people don't leave home and not come back.

Seven days after he'd gone missing, on 21st October my sister and I had been scheduled to go to River Island with the FLO, Ms Little, to go and buy the same purple shirt that Ricky had been wearing the night he was attacked, the aim being to use it in a reconstruction to help find him. The Missing Persons case was to be featured on London Tonight that day. My parents had gone out to the Monitoring Group, which was then situated in Southall, to participate in a press release to appeal for any information that could lead to Ricky's whereabouts, as at that time he was still missing. We wanted to know more about the racial attack and who had been involved, to try and develop leads into his disappearance.

I was sitting in the living room with my older sister and my younger brother and my cousin and my aunt, waiting for the FLO to arrive. Out of the window I saw a police car pull up outside at some speed across the driveway. This was no surprise. I was expecting them to arrive to take us to River Island but the speed at which they pulled up was odd. Ms Little and a PC came out of the car. At the time I was on the telephone to my mum on the landline by the window as she had rung me. Ms Little came in and she told me I had to hang up the phone. I told her I was on the phone to my mum and I couldn't hang up and she pulled the telephone wire out from the wall socket disconnecting the call. I was terrified. It all got serious very quickly. I was 17 years old at the time and my 11-year-old brother was also in the room.

Ms Little told us in the coldest way possible that they had found my brother's body "at the bottom of the river". I can't even begin to describe the shock that I felt. It is beyond words. Those words that she spoke are forever burned into my memory and as much as I would rather forget them, they replay in my memory all the time. "We found your brother's body at the bottom of the river." My brother was not a body, he was Ricky, my brother. When did he become a 'body'????

Trying to take control of the situation, I asked if she knew it was definitely him and she told me that they found his wallet next to him in the water. I had an asthma attack but not one of those two officers present bothered to help me. I had to crawl upstairs to go and get my inhaler after waving my arms to seek assistance of the two police officers failed. My 11-year-old brother was in bits and was confused. My sister was distraught. My cousin was in pieces and we were trying to translate to my aunt, in Punjabi, what we had just been told. At the time all I could think about was my parents, and did they know? My mum had not been well and I was worried that the shock would be too much for her and that I would lose her too. And I remember after taking my inhaler, sitting at the foot of the stairs waiting for her to come home, to just know that she was alive. Moments later, my parents came in the door and what followed cannot be described. Even just thinking about it is too hard.

My memory is imperfect because my mind does not want to remember. It comes in flashes, and moments. Almost like still images taken on a camera rather than a continuous moment. She came through the front door; we were in pieces. We hugged each other on the stairs. I was pleading with her to be okay. To live. For us. I don't know how long we were there for but I remember seeing my dad come in. He could not walk; he could not talk. He looked different, not like my dad, but a broken person. My dad on that day lost not only a son but a good friend also. They both worked on projects together and you could hear their laughter and arguments about different ways to do the job in hand. Our lives changed from that moment and have never been the same. I have changed and I will never be the person I was supposed to be; that I thought I would be. You change yourself, and build a life around it. It shapes you and you cannot control it.

What followed was years and years of campaigning to get to the truth and that quest for the truth continues. I will not be complete until we know what happened to Ricky that day. Family life changed forever. We remained and still remain very close but our lives changed irrecoverably. My mum became a campaigner, my dad spent all his time driving her to meetings, bringing her home, cooking her meals, looking after us. I looked after my little brother as though he were my child. We ran the campaign from home and from the Monitoring Group Office. When I wasn't doing my A levels, I spent my spare time writing speeches, collating campaign documents, going to meetings with my mum, attending meetings with our solicitor and the police. I suppose you could say that it gave me the drive at a time when I was really confused about what I wanted to do after completing my A levels, to do a law degree and go on to become a lawyer. It's funny that tragedy can shape your future at times in a positive way. I became a lawyer. My brother and sister went on to complete their degrees, my brother did a degree in criminology. The Police Missing Persons guidelines were changed as a direct result of Ricky's case. We've gone on to help and support other families who have sadly experienced events similar to what we experienced. We've tried to become a part of the wave for change to ensure that what we experienced doesn't repeat itself again and again.

Ricky was not like me. We were different but close. It's easy to say when someone has passed away that they were a good person, but Ricky truly was. He would never hurt anyone deliberately. He wanted to live quietly but successfully, and he lived his life achieving but not bragging, learning but not feeling entitled. He was my parent's son, our brother, a loyal friend and so much more with the potential to have lived a full life and have given so much back to others.

When I went to see Ricky in the morgue it finally hit home to me that he was gone forever. My big brother, the person I had looked up to my entire life, who I aspired to be a bit more like, (less selfish, more focused), who I could always rely on, who was consistent, who hardly ever went out, was dead. I'd never see that smile again, he'd never tease me again, he would never ask me for fashion advice again, and I wouldn't get to see how his life would play out. He wouldn't get to see what I achieved. I had always wanted to make him proud; his approval was worth having and mattered to me. His loss left me feeling unanchored, adrift. I lost my brother, and I lost any semblance of a normal family life for a long time. Even now I catch myself wondering, wouldn't things be different if Ricky was here? Wouldn't I be different? There is always and forever something missing. Someone is missing. He was truly one of the best people I have known. And he deserved to have lived on, got that dream job, got that degree, had a family, all the things that we have been blessed to go on and achieve.

There will never be a time where I don't feel his loss. At my wedding I felt his absence. I didn't have my big brother next to me to do all the things that a Big Brother is supposed to do. At my graduation I felt his loss. When I had my children, it saddened me that they would never know their uncle. I speak to them about him and I share his photos and videos with them so that they know what a truly amazing person he was.

My children are truly inspired by my mother, their grandmother. They know she is an inspirational woman who will always speak the truth. They see her as a strong woman, and every time they see her on the TV or see a picture in a press cutting, they are so very proud of who their grandmother is, as am I and I know that Ricky would be so proud of my mother because one of the things he always used to laugh and joke about was how my mother would never take 'no' for an answer. He'd be so proud about how his younger brother and how his sisters have lived their lives. He would've been delighted to have met his nephews and nieces, he would've been proud of how his family, including his uncles and aunts and all of his cousins, who were all very close to him, rallied round to support us when he was missing and after he died.

Losing a sibling is devastating and unnatural. We lived our lives honestly, working hard, studying hard, never getting into trouble, never expecting trouble to derail our lives in the way that it has, to take away, forever, a brother, a son. Yet here we are, less happy than we might have been, forever changed, never quite the same, always with someone missing. It is a hard way to live but my family and I try to move forward with Ricky forever in our memory and in our hearts. We think about him, we talk about him and we continue to love him.

It hurts to see my parents suffer so much. They are good people who did not deserve this. No one deserves this. All their lives they have never hurt anyone, and have always tried to do good by others. But we cannot change what has happened. Going forwards, looking to the future, as that is all we have, we will not stop, I will not stop, till we find out what happened to Ricky, and till the police and his killers are held accountable. Even now, more than 25 years after his loss, we are made aware of families who are being treated the way that we were. Their loved ones are being brutally killed and the police are not doing enough to get to the truth. We don't expect miracles. We just want the police to do their job. We want the people who did this to be held accountable.

W-e w-i-l-l n-o-t s-t-o-p.

This is a poem I wrote on the day of Ricky's funeral. I hope it expresses what I struggle to express to anyone, and at times, even myself:

Left in a Cold Grave

Left in a cold grave
Beneath the alien sea
Neglected in your undeserving state
A victim of man's lack of civility
Simply a tragic accident to the rest of the world
An unwelcome weight upon the conscience of humanity
 Left in a cold grave
Forgotten for a week even by me.

Left in a cold grave
Pleading to be given peace
Lamenting at the fate thrust upon you
Why should life given so recently so suddenly cease
Left in a cold grave
Forced to surrender life's lease.

Left in a cold grave
Fossilised by the mud in which you lay
With thoughts of your family left behind to haunt you
Wondering how much longer in this darkness you must stay
Left in a cold grave
Whilst your dignity was steadily washed away.

Left in a cold grave
waiting to be discovered
Helpless to tell those who search desperately for you
The life they search for will never be recovered
Left in a cold grave
Whilst those who stole your life remain blissfully

undiscovered.

Left in a cold grave
Your cries for help unanswered must remain
Helpless to walk again into my arms
Helpless to ease my pain
Left in a cold grave
Unable to explain

Left in a cold grave
Your lips cold and silent too
Unable to tell others who thought it an accident
That their assumptions were untrue
Left in a cold grave
Who stole your life away from you!

Left in a cold grave
Beneath the alien sea
Neglected in your undeserving state
A victim of man's lack of civility
Simply a tragic accident to the rest of the world
An unwelcome weight upon the conscience of humanity
Left in a cold grave
Forgotten for a week even by me.

Chapter 3

Finding Ricky and the Funeral

No more will I see your glowing smile
No more will I hear your key in the door
Sleep well dear son, be at peace at last
Wait for me, and we'll be together forever more.

Travelling home from the Monitoring Group, having just been told Ricky was dead, was a panic-stricken journey drenched in dread. How was I going to break this news to my children? They loved their brother. I was grasping for words to tell them he had left us forever. There were none.

I had promised to bring Ricky home and now I had broken that promise. I felt guilty as I believed I had destroyed my children's faith in me. How was I going to face my children now?

My mind visited the night Ricky left home seven days ago as if I was watching a movie. I had cooked dinner and we were both laughing as I told him he had to finish it. He said he wasn't a baby, but I told him he will always be my baby. Now my baby is no longer here.

The car stopped outside my house and Balwant helped me get out. It was the same building but looked unutterably changed and my children were waiting for me. It took a few minutes to register all of this. Why was I alive when my son was dead?

Throat constricted, unable to breathe, I stumbled through the front door 15-20 minutes after leaving the Monitoring Group.

Balwant, after having got me home, couldn't function. We were a family, shattered and broken.

I looked at my children and their faces. There was so much pain, and anguish in there I just wanted to die. I did not want to see their eyes full of tears and full of questions. I was willing for death to come to me because I could not comfort any of them.

I noticed two police officers standing in my lounge. I was given a second round of devastating news!

My daughters told me that while I was on the telephone with them, Ms Little, the Family Liaison Officer, told them to end my call, and to switch off the television.

I thought the FLOs were trained in breaking bad news to the family. If there were any circumstance where such expertise might be put into practice, this was certainly one of them.

However, this Family Liaison Officer decided not to wait for me, even though she knew I was headed home. She took it upon herself to tell my children that their brother's body had been discovered at the bottom of the river.

To this day I still don't know why she did this, or who gave her permission to *add this insult to injury*.

I tried to go near my 11-year-old son, who just flinched and moved away from me. He was like a statue, not moving, not making eye contact, not talking, A statue standing in front of me. There was an odd look in his eyes. He was elsewhere. He did not want to come near me, and he kept looking at the police officers. Seeing all my children broken on that day shattered my heart and mind eternally.

I found my elder daughter just standing there with glasses of water on a tray, her eyes pleading with me to tell her this news was wrong. She was on autopilot, offering drinks to everyone because she didn't know what else to do.

I was told that the police (after devastating my children) continued to talk and joke among themselves. None of them decided to comfort them or ensure they were okay.

My 17-year-old daughter had an asthma attack directly in front of them. She could not talk and was waving her arms in the air to attract help. Even then none of them paid any attention. My daughter had to crawl up the stairs to get her inhaler. She could have died that day too.

Drained and detached, my mind refused to believe the news about Ricky. Even though I was in the room, I was absent. I thought my head would explode from the thunder in my mind. I was becoming angry. I felt ashamed in front of my children. I felt I had not been able to keep my promise to them and also I had not been there when the police broke this news about their brother's death to them. How did this happen? I then remembered when at work I was dealing with a case where the parents had young children. We needed some information and I wondered whether I could ask a child. I was told by my boss that only the social workers, trained to deal with children, will ask this question in the presence of their parents. I now ask why the police were not aware of this. There was fear, more like panic inside me that my children will never trust me again. But I am glad to say that my children are sensible and know that this decision was taken out of my hands by the police. I had no say in this.

Nobody had the right to give this devastating news my children, and then in my absence too. The news was mine to tell. It was my role to break it to them in a way I thought they could handle. How dare the police deprive me of a mother's right to deliver delicate information regarding the death of my son to his siblings.

I told the police officers to leave my home after the damage they had done to my family. Not only had I lost Ricky but my three remaining children were distraught and in pieces. In my emptiness I hugged them, tried to talk to them but had no words to comfort them. I felt drained and all hollow inside and when I did try to speak, I could not remember any words and it was too painful to speak. I left the children with Balwant who was also not aware of what was going around him. I went upstairs unable to do anything more. I stumbled a couple of times on the stairs before reaching Ricky's room and locked the door.

I needed to scream and shout but was unable to do so in front of the children. I laid on Ricky's bed with his jumper clutched to my heart and willed for death. Ricky was alone and I wanted to join him.

I wanted to escape. I was incapable of dealing with this searing pain which was tearing my body apart. I wanted to disappear forever.

Somehow I felt hands pulling me out. I felt Ricky's presence and saw his face. I felt a tremor of love and courage enter my body. It pulled me off the bed and suddenly I was standing. I went to the bathroom, vomited, splashed cold water on my painful swollen eyes and changed clothes.

The clothes I had been wearing belonged to a woman who had failed to find Ricky, her own son, and had let him and his family down and I did not deserve to be a mother. What kind of mother am I? These lines kept on playing in my mind. I tried to shut these out but they persisted

A meek little woman was not going to find who killed her son. I had to shed a mother's role and become someone else. I had to become a Campaigner. I needed to put my shyness away and become a voice that would be listened to.

I went downstairs to meet my children. A lot of people were in the sitting room. Somebody mentioned that Ricky must have been beaten and thrown into the water. Hearing this I collapsed. Inderjeet, my younger brother, who, together with Suresh, had been driving us all around since Ricky went missing, picked me up from the floor and put me into bed. Marion, my friend went with my daughter to pick up medication prescribed by my doctor, who had caught word of Ricky's death. After that, I don't remember much of what happened except somebody put me in bed.

My request to see Ricky was refused as he was taken to the mortuary for a post-mortem.

Officer Morgan, the one who introduced himself as 'Consultant' in charge of the investigation, reappeared at the house after Ricky was recovered, telling us his death was just a tragic accident. This was before the post-mortem was even completed.

Mr Morgan reached his decision because Ricky's trouser buttons were undone, and that in his opinion, Ricky went to the river to urinate, fell in and died instantly.

As I will relate further into this book, there are so many reasons why this assumption is so flawed. I was sure that someone had prevented Ricky from returning home. I could not understand why he never returned home. His phone and jacket were in the friends' car but he had £30 in his pocket, on his person, for either a bus fare or enough money for a cab. He had withdrawn £30 from Barclays Bank that day and had a receipt to confirm this. He was close to a bus stop so what prevented him from boarding the bus? He was used to public transport and cabs so someone prevented him from coming home.

His friends were talking of going on to the night club just before the attack, so Ricky knew that they would not be in the car. There was no reason why Ricky would walk back to Down Hall Road towards the car where the police just assumed, without evidence, it is where he went before entering the water. The car did not belong to him and he did not have the keys to it. I said this to the police but I was ignored. We went into the bank to speak to the manager to see if there was a camera attached to the ATM which could give us more information but unfortunately there was no camera. Even if I follow the police theory, the car was not parked very close to the river. If Ricky wanted to urinate he would have done it near the car among the bushes and not walk right to the river and relieve himself knowing there were people in the boats nearby who could easily see him. As everybody who knew Ricky had stated that he was shy and would not embarrass himself to go the edge of the river to urinate. A convenient story created to close the case!

My family went to see Ricky the next day in the mortuary. Throughout the numb journey, I was praying it might be a mistake. It would be somebody else there.

I was the first person to see Ricky. I had to identify my son. Sure enough, it was my Ricky lying there. He looked as if he had come out of a sauna with his shining black hair and his skin which also shone and looked so fresh.

I heard gut-wrenching screams, looked around to see where these dreadful screams were coming from. I then realised they were coming from my mouth; sounds I did not understand as I had never heard anything like this before. Then I heard Balwant's cries. He had followed me into the room after hearing my cries. Balwant was my rock and I needed to be strong for him too. I could not see him in such pain and tried to hold my emotions in check. Almost immediately everyone who had accompanied us joined us in the room. Everybody was distressed, some openly crying, some trying to hide their sobs. Time stood still. Nobody spoke. All I could see was Balwant crying and holding me, family and supporters holding tissues on their eyes and mouths. My mind was swirling around in circles. My eyes saw Ricky but my mind was screaming that it cannot be Ricky. My son cannot die and leave me and his family. I did not want to leave him. He was wearing a gown with a pretty lace around his neck. I touched him and asked him if he was cold. I tucked him with the blankets he already had on him—in case he felt cold

I then put my hand on my son's forehead and prayed for him to always stay by my side and I promised him justice. My words were clear and loud. I told him that as long as I have life, I will try to find his murderers and get him justice. This promise is still engraved on my heart. This promise gives me courage when I feel I begin to fall into that black hole of depression and unfathomable loss again.

I was told that Ricky was ready to be moved to a Chapel of Rest of our choice and we could sign all the relevant forms and move him. I was given his clothes and told that if a family asks for clothes they are washed and given to them. But if I wanted to wash them myself, I could take them home right away and I did.

When we left that day, upon collecting his clothes, we made it clear that we were going to arrange for an independent post-mortem which was later carried out.

My husband and I tried to see Ricky as often as we could in the Chapel of Rest. My brother would take us, and I would sit and talk to Ricky, telling him that his two brothers, who I had lost as babies, were already there waiting for him and would look after him. He should not feel lonely. I knew time was limited and precious, so I talked about his siblings, how they were feeling and how much they missed him, who came to see us and what they said. I just talked and talked knowing that after his cremation, I would not be able to see him. I wanted to keep him, delay the cremation but also knew it was not possible or fair to Ricky and my family. Family, relatives and friends used to come to our house every day to pay their respects as is in our tradition. Most of the time I used to escape them by going to the Chapel to see Ricky.

The day of the funeral was a blur. Everyone rushed around trying to arrange a funeral for my son. It was surreal.

I kept myself busy talking to the undertaker about what kind of service we wanted, arranging flowers, Gurdwara (temple) bookings, service and lunch etc. Balwant and Mon did most of it. Balwant's sister and my siblings, family, all helped us.

Relatives and supporters continued to come to our house and the door was always open. Ricky's school and university friends came over. I was an automaton, a robot who continued to talk, listen to people, drank endless cups of tea, went to bed and woke up when I was told. Somebody else was inhabiting my body and I did not exist anymore. I was no longer me. I ceased to exist and at times also forgot my name. I remember my mother shaking me and asking why I did not answer her as she had been talking to me for a long time. I did not hear her. I was in another world, my world with Ricky, just the two of us.

Ricky was cremated on 3 November 1997.

3 November 1997 was the day when I said goodbye to my son forever. Not able to kiss his forehead ever again, never to talk to him or hug him. My children had chosen Ricky's clothes to wear at his funeral the night before. It was their parting gift to their brother, the brother they will never see again.

My husband and I sat up all night, each one of us engrossed in our own thoughts, trying to spare each other's pain by just losing ourselves in memories of our son and wondering whether we had the courage to carry his coffin and to say a final farewell the next day. We did not say much to each other as each of us was dreading the next day. Do we have courage to do this? How does a parent say good bye to their child? How does a parent carry out a coffin of their child from their home? How do we then comfort our children and answer their endless questions? Each one telling the other to go to bed but unable to get up to go to bed. Our children went to sleep and we sat near them watching them. How will they react tomorrow? Will they be able to cope? How can I now protect them? Endless questions going in our minds. How can the last time Ricky enters and leaves this home, his home, that he helped build with his own hands, be in a coffin?

None of us was prepared for it, no one wanted to do it, but we knew we had to go through this last step for Ricky. We had to say goodbye. We had to carry him out of our house forever, the house he had helped us build and he was proud of it. Now I am unable to part with this house because this is the last place where Ricky lived. I feel as long as I am in this house, Ricky is around me.

I dressed up for the funeral as I did not want to let Ricky down. He was particular about clothes. He had bought me a green and a red suit to wear on his 18th birthday, one year and a half earlier. He chose red, saying it suits my personality.

He did not like me wearing white because it lacked colour and he did not want to see me without colour in my life.

I had to wear white clothes at the funeral. How Ricky must have hated them! It is our tradition to wear white.

I knew I needed to be brave as Ricky had always admired my strength, which by this time had ebbed away, but somehow, I kept on going. I tried to push everybody and everything out of my mind to get through the day.

My front garden was full to the brim with flowers brought to us by lots of people including strangers. I quickly put on my mask, a mask of courage, as I did not want to show people that I was broken up inside. I had to be strong for my Ricky, he relied on me as well as my other children.

Although very distressed, Balwant, together with the family, saw to our guests, with his eyes tracking and following me, making sure I was ok.

Imprints of Ricky

Looking around the house Ricky was everywhere. Imprints of Ricky embedded in the TV speakers he had hung, the wall he helped build, the woodwork he had varnished, and his treasured computer.

The kitchen brickwork he did when he carried the bricks to the roof to pass them to his dad. The patio he dug up, which resulted in blisters on his hands.

A surprise car (an old one was always breaking down) we had bought for his 21st birthday was still in the garage screaming for him to jump into it and drive. And then again, I looked at his computer. He taught me to use a computer, and he laughed at me, telling me to concentrate.

His spotless room where the paint was still fresh. He had boasted he would paint the whole house once he had finished his room.

His clothes were all folded and hung in the wardrobe as if

he would walk back in and pick up where he left off.

Instead, he would be carried out, lifeless, in a wooden box. His treasured computer calling him back but Ricky was oblivious to everyone's cries.

We got dressed to welcome our son home for the last time. Prayers were said for Ricky while waiting for the coffin to arrive. Media and a crowd of people came to our house. I did not recognize some of them, but there was concern and love on their faces and flowers in their hands. My son's coffin arrived home. It was an open casket, and everybody rushed to see him.

Some put flowers in the casket. I was thinking of all the excuses I could make up to keep him home a bit longer. My children all put small, special items in the coffin with Ricky. It was to shows Ricky he was very much loved and not alone.

My youngest son wanted to keep the good memories and instead of seeing Ricky wrote a letter to his brother and placed it in the coffin. It was his way of saying farewell. He was not able to deal with Ricky's death. He thought he could still conjure up his memories of Ricky if he did not see him in his coffin. I respected his decision.

I wanted my children to become whole again. But where do I start? What do I need to do? Seeing my daughters sobbing in the corner broke my heart but I was also broken up and did not have the energy to console them. I was numb. The strongest love is the love of a parent for their child, so the loss of a child is the worst pain a parent can feel. It was effort to move my body and I mainly existed on pain killers. They gave relief to my physical pain as each and every part of my body was painful, as if it was also angry and screaming for some respite. This respite has not entered my life for the last 25 years.

My younger daughter wanted to see Ricky, but when she did, she, like all of us, was shocked by how much his body had deteriorated. Little did we know, the police had undertaken a post-mortem (another one) before the funeral without our knowledge. Balwant embraced her and took her into the kitchen. She needed to recover from the shock. She still has nightmares about this.

As per our tradition, after Ricky was brought home in a casket, then we went to the Gurdwara (temple) where Ricky's casket was also taken. We said prayers and then went onto the crematorium which was full, with people spilling outside.

We carried our son's coffin on our shoulders. My husband and I carried the front of the coffin and our family carried the rest. Not many women at that time carried a coffin but I did as

A newspaper report of Ricky's funeral

I gave him birth and told him I was sending him away because I had no other choice. That coffin felt heavy because I filled it with all my love and put my heart and soul in it as well. He was not alone, he had a part of me with him. So I walked with the others, one foot after another, I was in a sort of trance.

When I was asked to press the button for the casket to move forward at the end of the funeral, I was reluctant at first as I thought I was killing my own son. I looked at Balwant and his eyes were pleading with me as the same thoughts were also in his mind. I was like a statute and unable to move or say anything. Inderjeet, my younger brother, then hugged me and took me near the casket. His strong arms were around me as he knew my legs were shaking and I had difficulty in standing up. I took a deep breath, closed my eyes and pressed the button together with Balwant. I had sent my son away from me forever and I felt all hollow inside. My mind was screaming that I will no longer be able to feel him or see him.

I told Ricky he was not alone, a part of me was also in his coffin. I was sending him to his grandparents and his two younger brothers. Though one tragedy does not prepare you for the next, they could look after each other. This thought gave me some peace.

We then went back to the Gurdwara where more prayers were said and lunch was served. This is a Sikh tradition. I still don't know how I coped and what exactly happened. I just did what I was told or what was expected of me. I recall lots of people came to me to express their sympathy but I don't remember what I said to them. People's faces were swimming in front of my eyes but my mind did not register anything. All I could see was Ricky lying in his coffin. My children were present throughout the funeral but I don't remember seeing them. I think my family was looking after them. I had no energy and nothing to give to my children. My arms and legs were moving but I was numb.

Everybody returned home after the funeral except my Ricky. I had told him as he lay in his coffin, that I could not take him home as my heart had wanted to. The friends and family then left and finally we were on our own.

I did not know how to console Balwant and my children. We both tried to be brave for our children, but something was eating us alive. I suppose it was grief, and not knowing how to live a life without Ricky. Endless questions were going around in our minds to which we had no answers.

I was restless, angry, exhausted, and hurt, and compelled to get justice for my son, cremated at just 20 years old. One or two people commented that it was fate but I became angry hearing this. What fate? Why this fate? My anger helped me to push back against fate, to tell myself that however low I get, I will not stay down. I will look the world in the eye and to hell with anyone who doesn't want to look back. I created my own world, a world which I knew would be full of grief and I knew that I would just need to close my ears to some comments that I did not want to hear and continue with my fight for justice overcoming all the obstacles in my way. But at that time I did not know the heavy price I would have to pay to take on the authorities and to challenge them. And I have been vocal about Ricky's race attack, his death and the treatment of authorities ever since.

With John McDonnell MP

On 30 November 1997 we went to Plymouth and took a boat to Cornwall to scatter Ricky's ashes in the sea. I hugged the urn and thought, was this all that was left of my handsome 5'8" son? It was a long drive and everybody wanted to hold the urn, I suppose we all knew that after this we will not be able to hold any part of Ricky. I was reluctant to give this to anybody else but thought each and every one of us was hurting and Ricky belonged to us all. So we took turns to hold Ricky's remains and prayed God to let him rest in peace. At least he had gone where nobody will hurt him again.

Inderjeet knowing how much I was hurting, rushing to go near River Thames, then running away from it had picked Cornwall as he knew I did not want to scatter Ricky's ashes back into the River Thames as we had done with our relatives.

Cornwall was a beautiful place, the sea was calm and we

all took turns to scatter his ashes. Ricky was gone, my arms were empty and all I had was my promise to him. This promise which keeps me alive.

On the return journey to shore everybody was quiet, lost in our own thoughts, each one of us finally realising that Ricky was gone, we would never see him again. Even then my brain was refusing to believe that my Ricky was dead. A parent should never have to say a final goodbye to a child. No parent should have to carry their child's coffin.

After Ricky's funeral, life went on and we were pulled along with it. The children returned to school and Balwant went to work. I was in no fit state to return to my employment and took six months off in an attempt to help heal.

But rest for my body and soul was not in sight. I was constantly on the road to meetings, conferences, and doing interviews with the press. I kept myself busy and hoped that someone would eventually speak up to tell us what happened that night and how Ricky had met his death.

After meetings I would come home exhausted and crawl into bed. Most of the time I vomited when I returned home. Sheer exhaustion, heart and body full of grief and not eating properly because there was too much to do was playing havoc with my health. Any time I did eat, I felt guilty because I was getting nourishment while my son was probably hungry.

I was unable to deal with the tension and grief. I would set Ricky's place on the dining table and call him to eat his food. He would never come.

I closed his bank account and took over the contract for his mobile telephone. I kept his telephone with me all the time and it became a norm for me. There was a recorded message from Ricky on the phone which I listened to many times a day.

I spent a lot of time in The Monitoring Group dealing with paperwork regarding the campaign. Lots of people sent letters and phoned with constant questions as to why the police were not dealing with this case properly.

Life continued but I was just existing and not really living.

In time I learnt to put a mask on my face, the mask which showed people I was strong and coping with Ricky's death but I was slowly crumbling inside.

Balwant and I became good at hiding our sorrows from each other as each of us were protecting the other and trying to protect our other children who desperately needed us.

Once or twice when outside walking I thought I had seen Ricky and I would run to that person. I can't describe my disappointment when it wasn't him.

I started to take each day as it came and never made any plans for the future as I was too frightened to be hurt again.

I was grateful for all the support I had received during the first few weeks as I would not have coped.

After nearly 25 years, it still does not feel real. I keep on imagining that I will hear Ricky's key in the door and "how are you mum" as soon as he enters the door.

After the funeral I thought I could not possibly be hurt more but...

Chapter 4

Birth of the Justice for Ricky Reel Campaign

In moments when I felt alone and forlorn, a mere shadow in the world
Without my son, in a dark, cold room, locked behind a heavy door
A stranger has reached out and uttered words of kindness and hope
And I realise Ricky, you and I are not alone, anymore

When Ricky died, a huge part of me died along with him. What was I to do now? I was a mother, without her son. I had an empty bedroom in my home, his car undriven in the garage, his clothes unworn, his voice forever silent and a huge void in my life that had, before this, been full. Did I start the Campaign for Justice for my son to fill that void? No. Did I do it to fill my time? No. I did because there seemed no other way open to my family and I to get to the truth of what had happened to Ricky.

If there had been any other route, if the police had simply done what they were supposed to do, I would not have had to campaign for justice, as there would be no need to have this need. "Need" is the true reason why the Campaign was born.

There was a need for justice because Ricky's life was worth

something, and although I was now forced to live in a world without him, I could not live in a world with my other children where justice was denied based on someone's race, our race. It simply was not an option.

From the day Ricky went missing, we were advocating and campaigning to get to the truth of what happened. We didn't call it a Campaign because we didn't even know what we were doing. At the time, we were just putting one foot in front of the other, seeking answers, seeking information, seeking the truth.

We printed leaflets appealing for information, we arranged a press conference, we walked the streets looking for witnesses, clues and CCTV and we appealed to the police over and again to take his disappearance seriously.

When Ricky was found, we continued these efforts, but we found that more and more people were coming forward wanting to help us, support us, because they could see who was wrong.

It was that the police were more concerned with shutting us down than finding out what had happened to Ricky. We knew we had been wronged, but to see others recognise this too helped us realise that we were not alone, and there is a great deal of strength in that.

I remembered the promise I had made when I saw Ricky in the morgue the day after we found out that he was dead: to get Justice. I knew I could not quietly resume my life as it had been before Ricky's death. I have seen a number of deaths like Ricky's over the years, and grieving families. People deal with it differently, and there is no right or wrong way to face grief and loss. But for me, I saw that it would be a betrayal of Ricky and all that his life meant, and of my own beliefs, if I did not seek out justice.

In the office of SMG, the Justice for Ricky Reel Campaign was born, out of necessity, to seek justice.

I met John McDonnell and Suresh Grover with Balwant, Mon and a few work colleagues. These colleagues had stood with me in my hour of need and they are still with me

We sat in Suresh's office and each one of us expressed our

own commitment to find out what had happened to Ricky, and ideas of how to achieve this. Mon put £50 into the Campaign to kick start the collection of donations as we knew that we needed funds to cover legal and campaigning costs. These included printing of leaflets, posters, brochures, photographs, and basic stationary costs. There was no other source of funding available to us.

Suresh, John, my family and friends helped me launch The Campaign for Justice for Ricky Reel with a large Public Meeting at the offices of the Southall Monitoring Group, and it was attended by about 150 people on 17 January 1998. Mr Lawrence, the father of Stephan Lawrence was our guest. It was the first real public meeting for Ricky Reel and I was overwhelmed by the support from people who were strangers then and are now close friends. The strange thing about death is that it has a way of bringing people together.

I addressed my first public meeting at a time when the emotions were so raw, having only lost Ricky three months earlier. It was terrifying initially but I knew I had to speak otherwise no one would ever know what had happened to my son and no one would help us get justice for him

Like so many steps that were taken that would shape the Justice for Ricky Reel Campaign in the years to come, they were taken because if we didn't take these steps, who would, because it became increasingly clear the police had let us down and could not be relied upon in our case to take Ricky's case on and investigate it properly.

I was nervous at this meeting, and I wrote a few lines on a scrap of paper because my thoughts were running faster than my words. Before I started speaking I looked at Balwant's face and felt that both of us really needed to know the truth and speaking about Ricky and the police failures and appealing for help was the only way forward for us and Ricky. Balwant's eyes were giving me courage.

It was hard to address a room full of people who are looking at you. But in those faces I saw so much solidarity, such a willingness to support our family, that with each spoken word I gained courage and conviction.

I forgot the paper and all my love for my son embraced me and when I finished, I couldn't even remember speaking. My mind had carried me away to a place where I was a Campaigner, not only a mother. I quickly went to hug my little 11-year-old son as he had been sitting there, watching me, looking lost. He still sometimes has that look when he is in deep thought and thinks nobody is looking at him, but I feel his pain. He had lost his big brother, the one who played football with him, the one he looked up to, the one who would tease him and make him laugh. How does an 11-year-old understand loss? The loss so brutally told to him by the police, the loss that turned his world upside down, the loss that changed him, the loss that stole his

childhood, the loss where a word "death" was mentioned but no comfort or compassion was shown, the loss that would haunt him forever. The loss that turned him from a child into an adult in a blink of an eye

Suresh coordinated and carried out the searches for Ricky and witnesses. Later he would help us to contact the media, arrange pickets, lobbying for a proper investigation into Ricky's death. John equally would become instrumental, raising this case in the House of Common to liaising with police and other members of Parliament.

Sometimes people think a "campaign" is something families casually decide to develop. In our case it was the only option, a movement of desperation, not a choice.

My new life as a campaigner began. It was very daunting but it was something I had to do. It was impossible to be both a mother and a campaigner all of the time. I really wanted to be a mother to the rest of my children as it was a traumatic and life-changing time for them too, but I had made a promise to Ricky. He was also my child. I felt torn between my other children, who were here, and my son who was ripped from my life.

As a family, we decided that I would devote my time to the Campaign and Balwant would look after our children when I was away from home. Balwant attended most of the meetings with me whenever possible as the children were still in school.

With Neville Lawrence at the launch of the Campaign

We tried to return some normality to our children's lives and continued to make joint decisions.

The Justice for Ricky Reel Campaign took off quickly but has been through many different phases. In the early years before social media was active it took many forms

We had many meetings with the police, with our lawyers

seeking answers and holding them to account where things had gone wrong. We organised peaceful pickets and protests. All of this was foreign to me and I was learning on my feet. Whenever we had arranged any protests we made sure that the police were informed of this. We had security in place and we told our supporters that we did not want any trouble and as a result our all events were always peaceful.

In November 1997 our family contacted a solicitor as we were not getting anywhere with the police. From then on we were legally represented by a Ms Louise Christian, our solicitor, who had a wealth of experience in dealing in cases such as Ricky's.

As a family we made a complaint against the Metropolitan Police's handling of Ricky's death to date. We met the officers from the Police Complaints Authority (which was what the current day Independent Police Complaints Commission was known as) with our solicitor in December 1997, and on 16 December 1997 the Surrey Police commenced an investigation into the Metropolitan Police's botched initial investigation into Ricky's death.

The police investigation at the time of the Inquiry was not very active because they wanted to close it, telling us it was just an accident. The PCA wrote to me that my case would not be like the Stephen Lawrence case, which had occurred just a few years earlier, and the PCA said that whatever had gone wrong, they would put it right straight away. They said that lessons had been learned and the same mistakes would not be repeated in my case. I was reassured that it wouldn't just be a bureaucratic process of allocating blame.

A day before the initial meeting with the PCA team, my solicitor received a telephone call from the PCA and was told that the Metropolitan Police had distributed some leaflets in Kingston Town Centre and told Surrey Police that they would not let them investigate Ricky's death.

All the Surrey Police could do was to investigate the complaint against the Metropolitan Police. It was clear to me that what had happened was that as soon as we made the complaint the Metropolitan Police suddenly started distributing their own witness appeal leaflets in Kingston Town Centre, claiming that because the investigation was "live", Surrey Police's remit would have to be restricted to investigating our complaint into Ricky's death rather than also investigating his death, as we had wanted, having lost complete faith in the Metropolitan Police by that point.

The Campaign for Justice continued. My life got tangled up between two police divisions, the Metropolitan Police and the Surrey Police. I missed many family dinners, birthdays, was unable to take or pick up my young son from school or spend time with him, unable to help him with his homework or take him out. His sisters took over that role because I could not do both. We were a fractured family doing the best we could to keep on going with the rest of our lives doing what we thought was right for us.

This was our family's joint decision and we knew there would be sacrifices, money shortages, the children would have to do without quite a lot of things that they were accustomed to, and they would have to do without me.

I could not be with them after school many evenings like I used to be, nor many weekends. Even when I was home, I was running the Campaign from my home, which took up a lot of time but it was a decision we had made and we were committed to making it work the best we could, as we all wanted justice.

The approach the police had taken with me from the beginning was that I should not be asking questions. I am an Indian woman, (Sikh) and it was clear to me that the police at that time in 1997 did not expect to be challenged by Indians, let alone a Sikh woman. We were just expected to be grateful that the police had come out and spoken to us and opened a file on Ricky's case.

To expect an active, open-minded investigation was clearly too big a task from an Indian family from their point of view. The shock on some of those officers' faces when we asked questions, when we challenged what they told is etched clearly on my memory. They tried to placate and patronise us when we challenged them. Instead of looking at me when I spoke to them, they would look at Balwant, a man, and address their answers to him, and look straight past me in those early days. And during the Campaign we were confronted by this attitude over and over again, and so the Campaign rose to meet these challenges.

I took six months off work as I was physically and mentally a wreck. I was not able to continue with my job as a Homeless Persons Officer with a West London Local Authority. My employers were good, they understood the trauma I was going through. But in those six months instead of resting I travelled all over the country talking about my Campaign and gathering support.

*Louise Christian &
Suresh Grover*

I returned to work after six months and I worked during the day time and still continued to attend meetings, conferences, etc. in the evenings or weekends. Sometimes I did media interviews during my lunch break. I did one in my work canteen instead of having lunch. Another one in a park next to my office. There were many more such meetings. That was the only way I could let the world know about Ricky's case. I thought if I did not do this Ricky would be forgotten and the authorities would continue with the same practice, mocking Asian's people's race and their parents for taking control over their children's decision about their lives.

Running a family justice campaign is not a polished effort, from a shiny office with lots of time to devote to meetings, events and correspondence. It is about finding every spare minute you have in an already busy life, to reply back to all the kind well-wishers who took the time to write to me and express their support, to write a speech for a meeting, to attend meetings all over the UK, to read and respond to legal correspondence, keep up to date with the police investigations, to support other families in similar plights. At the same time there were many other families who had also lost loved ones and I was also supporting those families by attending their events. I know how lonely it is to fight alone. I had met the families of Stephen Lawrence, Christopher Alder, Michael Menson, Daniel Morgan, Cherry Groce, Joy Gardiner, Roger Sylvester, Trevor Monerville, Blair Peach, Harry Stanley and Zahid Mubarek. Sabina Rizvi. All of us struggling to get justice for our loved ones. Everyone needed support. I cannot afford to sit by and

see other families suffer the injustice and would go and support them. There is strength in numbers. I have known heartache and can feel their pain as well.

It is a hard, at times uphill battle, but all completely worth the struggle. We had not chosen to be placed in a situation where we had to demand justice because it had not been afforded to us, but we had decided that we would not accept it and that came with sacrifices, personal, financial, emotional and physical.

At each meeting I bared my soul and told people what we had suffered. Still now, the shock on people's faces and the sharp intake of breath as they hear what we and other families have endured is palpable. After each meeting I have to put myself back together again and somehow carry on with everyday life. Even after nearly 25 years I find it very painful to talk about Ricky and of the events leading to his death, but if I don't talk—who will?—how will I get justice? The pain and grief has now become my companion and I live with it.

I remember in those early years, Suresh and Balwant took turns to drive me to these meetings. I drove but was too exhausted to drive long distances. I had no idea when or whether I ate anything. Suresh or Balwant would pretend they were hungry to encourage me to eat. After one such long distance meeting we stopped at a motorway cafe to get a coffee. I was tired and could not keep my eyes open and shuffled to the

toilet. A man's shouts at the door made me realise it was the men's toilet.

Then there were nights when I was unable to sleep. My pillow was always wet with my tears in the mornings. Tears were always shed behind closed doors, away from the family, away from the supporters. They became my companion.

The exhaustion I felt was not the type to help me slip into peaceful sleep at night. It was a feeling that made me restless and unable to "switch off". I just could not rest, and I still can't. There was always more to be done—another meeting, a speech to write, an interview to attend. I lost a huge amount of weight unwittingly and at the time I couldn't see it, but now looking back at the photos I see I was gaunt and drawn.

As the Campaign gained momentum, my young son started making "Justice for Ricky Reel" badges at home after school, which we took to all our meetings and distributed. It was so sad, seeing my young child make badges with the face of my dead son on them, smiling back at him, but my younger son said he wanted to do "something" for his brother. He said it was his contribution towards his big brother's campaign. Perhaps it was to ease his trauma as well.

My children and friends helped with correspondence as people kept writing in to ask about the case and offering support or donations toward our legal or campaigning costs. This was

Banner demanding justice for Ricky on the front of the offices of the Monitoring Group in Southall

way before email became popular and all correspondence was still by stamp and letter, or at times, fax.

Mon and my children dealt with much of the complicated paperwork/enquiries as I barely had time to do it. Suresh and Louise dealt with the legal work. We worked as a team. It is said that grief either makes you or breaks you. It made my family stronger and more determined to find how Ricky died. The support from members of the public gave me strength and courage. Campaigns require resources, manpower and support. My Campaign gave me a voice to highlight my case.

My supporters gave me courage to stand up and confront all the authorities involved in my son's case.

My family should have been given an opportunity to grieve for Ricky in our own home and space, and we should have been able to rely on the police to do their job.

We were living with the feelings of shock, dismay, anger, hurt, guilt, not being believed, and panic.

We wanted to sit at home to deal with these feelings, hug each other, support each other and talk about Ricky. I wanted my mother's arms around me, comforting me but I knew that this would weaken me. It will come later, once I get justice for my son. One more heartache for me—my mother died on 21 December 2014 waiting for justice. She lost the will to live after the death of my brother. This is another example of mothers and of the empty life they face after a death of a child. My father was spared of this heartache as he had died on 18 October1990. I needed to be strong to walk this journey so I locked all my emotions in my heart, and did not want to show anyone that I was all broken up inside. I needed to show people that I was capable of running this campaign. But instead, we were forced out on the streets, the only way to find who killed Ricky and why. A lot of family time was lost, never to be reclaimed. I didn't even make any new memories with my children as I had left them at home to do a job the police should have done in the first place.

Inderjeet, had supported me by lifting me in his strong arms at times when I was unable to cope with this trauma and had collapsed. He was like my shadow who was always trying to protect me from everyone. At times when my body refused to cope and I had ended in hospital, he was the one phoning constantly to make sure I was well and looked after properly. One such day was when I returned home after spending a day in hospital. At the same time Inderjeet was seriously ill in another hospital. I was worried about him and was thinking of visiting him when suddenly the door opened wide and he stood there with a big grin on his face because I was ok and at home. I found out later that when he heard I was in hospital, he had phoned my niece and asked her to go to the hospital with his clothes and he had sneaked out of the hospital with her just to see me and our family. He risked his life for me. He was also fighting for justice for Ricky who he looked upon as his son. I kept on telling him to get better as I needed him with me to get justice for Ricky. But unfortunately he died a few weeks later holding my hand and still waiting for justice on 30 April 2013.

To cope with Ricky's loss and the pressures of the Campaign, I wrote poetry.

Many was the time I would come back from a public meeting after talking about Ricky and write a poem as I had no other outlet for the feelings speaking about him would evoke. As a young child I started writing poetry but was not serious about it. I started writing again when Ricky went missing and

The Justice for Ricky Reel badge that I wore

then onwards. I used this as my conversation with Ricky. I wrote whatever I was feeling, talking to Ricky as I wrote and I felt Ricky was with me all the time. A feeling which I still have. I felt I was taking out my anguish, my fingers flying on the keyboard, without any conscious thoughts but just pouring out my grief. Knowing that I was sitting in Ricky's chair and using his computer gave me comfort as I wrote.

People at meetings about Ricky's case would often approach me and they saw me as a "courageous woman", but that is not how I saw myself then or now. I have done what I had to do, not from courage but from an unwillingness to accept that I am powerless to effect change, and an unwillingness to accept that the police can simply file Ricky's case away in the "too late to do anything about it" drawer.

Courage alone is not enough. Families like mine need support, resources, people around them with experience of supporting families like mine. I was awarded the "Asian Woman of the Year Award" by Cherie Blair in 2001. I felt honoured but as I went home with the award I still felt empty because I still had not received justice for my son. I put the

Speaking at an NUS Black Students meeting

award on Ricky's table and told him that at last some of our struggles have been recognised.

The Campaign gained strength and a national presence and meanwhile the Surrey Police investigation, under the umbrella of the Police Complaints Authority (PCA), of my complaint into the Metropolitan Police's handling of the case continued. We hoped this would lead to answers.

This was an opportunity for the police to demonstrate a willingness at the very least to approach the case in a way that was neither racist nor closed minded

When the PCA Report came out, it was immediately apparent that what went wrong in the Lawrence case had gone wrong in our case too. Lessons had not been learned. The thick PCA Report investigating our complaint was given to us but only after we agreed to sign a solemn, binding and legally enforceable promise, called an Undertaking, that I would not show this Report to anyone including my own children.

I signed it because if I had not, it was made plain that the Report, which was several hundred pages long, would not be disclosed to me, and all I would receive was a summary five or six pages long.

Where was the justice in going through the complaints procedure, only for the outcome to be shrouded in secrecy, to protect the police's position? To this day, almost 25 years later, that report, which outlines many but not all of the Met police officer's failings and recommended disciplinary action against them, remains confidential.

In an age where the police should be operating with transparency and accountability, I cannot see what private (to the family) or wider public interest there is in this crucial Report remaining private.

Our MP John McDonnell, however, being the courageous and tenacious man that he is, read out parts of the report in the House of Commons on 20 October 1999, the two-year anniversary of Ricky's death, in a bid to help get answers to Ricky's death and learn lessons from it.[1] John highlighted the following important points:

> a) There were admitted failures in the original investigation of Ricky's death and in the way in which the Metropolitan Police service responded to our family.

> b) The culture of defensive secrecy that still pervades our policing system clearly undermined, and continues to undermine, the confidence of the Reel family in the capacity of the police to appreciate and respond to their needs.

> c) Police officers are employed to serve members of the public, but the refusal of the Metropolitan Police to operate openly and transparently during this investigation demonstrates that secrecy is still deeply embedded in the Metropolitan and that there is an

institutional reluctance to accept that the Metropolitan is the servant of the public and should therefore be accountable to the public that it is serving.

d) This continuing culture of secrecy also undermines the potential for building confidence in the Metropolitan Police following the Lawrence case and the Macpherson inquiry. The culture of secrecy is best exemplified in this case by the refusal of the Metropolitan Police to publish the Report of the inquiry of the Police Complaints Authority into its initial investigation of Ricky's death. The recommendations of the Macpherson report state clearly the need for openness and transparency.

In summarising some of the conclusions of the PCA report John stated:

e) In respect of communications with the Reel family during the initial police investigation, the need for clear, careful and considerate communication with the family was critical in investigations of that kind—as was learned from the Lawrence inquiry. In the investigation, we discovered that: "Each of them delivering slightly different messages. The report concluded: Mrs Reel and other members of the family were visited or contacted by telephone by a total of 10 different officers, from three different areas, in the space of two days".

f) The report states that the identification and interviewing of witnesses was vital to the lines of inquiry. It acknowledges that Mrs Reel herself identified and located some of the witnesses.

g) The inquiry also revealed that, in some instances, no records were checked by the Metropolitan Police to confirm or support witness accounts; cross-referencing of information did not take place; and some witnesses were not found until the PCA investigating team found them.

h) Witness information was sometimes not passed on from junior to senior officers.

i) The PCA report states that there were "no debriefings", which would have been "common in investigations of this nature; as a result, potentially important information was lost".

j) One of the things that it reveals is that property records at Kingston Police station showed that a videotape from British Rail at Kingston had been seized by a policeman and deposited in the property store. The tape was not viewed. Its existence was not drawn to the attention of investigating officers, and on 17 November 1997 the tape was destroyed... "The British Rail tape was indeed seized, not viewed and destroyed".

k) The PCA inquiry reveals that all video evidence from shops was not seized promptly enough to provide information.

l) The PCA states that videotapes from two restaurants may have provided information to the investigation had they been seized promptly, but they were not.

m) Regarding photographic evidence, the three friends of Ricky Reel were never shown any photos of known racist offenders or offenders who had previously been involved in racial incidents in the area, in an attempt to identify the youths involved in the racial attack on the group.

n) On forensic information, the PCA inquiry revealed that no clothing or personal items retrieved from Ricky's body were subject to forensic examination. Details of his clothing were not recorded and the PCA concluded: given the high priority accorded to the search for Ricky, the decision to call a special post-mortem and circumstances before his disappearance, the way in which forensic evidence was dealt with this is difficult to justify.

o) The key issue is that the investigation was into a missing person report, but that the link between the racial attack earlier in the evening and Ricky going missing was not made soon enough. Not only was insufficient forensic evidence taken, but, as the PCA states, it is hard to justify why independent expert judgement was not sought on some issues.

p) In the post-mortem, the report makes it clear that no one was clear about who was in control of the post-mortem examination and who should have been asking the right questions.

q) On verification at the scene, the report reveals that no forensic analysis was conducted at the area where it was assumed Ricky entered the river; no fingerprint examination was made of the railing nearby and no foliage was taken; and there was no examination of the concrete block, although photographs were taken. The report concludes that forensic examination of the bank would have been helpful: it might or might not have substantiated the claim that the incident was an accident, but it would at least have challenged that theory.

r) The PCA report states that a key element in the investigation was identifying the means of escape used by the earlier attackers. The inquiry highlighted the role of the No. 281 bus, which the attackers may well have boarded. The Metropolitan Police did not check the records of work or tickets on the No. 281. The report states that the No. 281 was "the most likely line of inquiry to lead to identification of the youths or other witnesses". The failure to follow up that line of inquiry was described as "a significant omission".

s) Overall, the report condemns the investigation because:

1. *it lacked focus;*

2. *it eliminated the racial incident earlier in the evening too readily;*

3. *it lacked thoroughness; and*

4. *there was a failure to initiate an early reconstruction of what happened that night.*

5. *There was also confusion over the ownership of the investigation of the racial incident.*

6. *The investigators came to the conclusion of accidental death before there was corroboration, and,*

7. *There was a failure to adopt policies that would have ensured that professional standards were maintained in the detail of the investigation.*

t) In addition, the inquiry set out in some detail a series of recommendations for the reform of policing practices, and the problem now is that those recommendations, commendable though they seem, are part of the PCA report, which the Metropolitan keeps secret. That completely misses the point of the Macpherson report into the Lawrence case. Public confidence can be restored and maintained in any public service only if mistakes, when they occur, are honestly admitted, and any remedial action is openly and honestly displayed.

In this instance, the failure to publish the PCA report means that we cannot allow for an honest admission of mistakes. More importantly, it provides no opportunity for the Metropolitan to display what lessons it has learned and what improvements have been made. It thus misses completely an opportunity to regain the confidence of the community in our police service.

Above are some, not all, of the points taken directly from the Hansard report. I will be forever grateful to John for raising parts of the Report in the House of Commons. If he had not, even these points which illustrate just *some* of the police's failings, and which are just the tip of the iceberg, would not have found their way to the public. The sad truth is, this is just a small representation of larger, and more pervasive, wrongs perpetrated by the police against us, and other families.

After this publication, we continued to campaign for justice for Ricky, and this included seeking an inquest with a jury and publication of the PCA Report, which remains confidential despite our efforts.

We approached trade unions for funding and they supported us in many ways. I have been a member of Unison myself for years before Ricky's death, as I believed strongly in the movement. The idea of justice and the strength and dignity of the common man was something my parents had instilled in me as a child.

I became part of a wider movement for justice, including the National Civil Rights Movement launched by the Monitoring Group.

I attended The Stephen Lawrence Inquiry chaired by Sir William Macpherson in 2000 at Hannibal House in Elephant and Castle. I was there on the first day and then onwards almost every day. Suresh always accompanied me and looked after me. It was painful to hear the evidence and sometimes uncomfortable sitting there listening to one excuse after another by the police. Many times I had to go to the toilet either to vomit or to hide my tears and sobs as I felt Stephen's parents' pain, the same pain that was destroying me as well. I felt their trauma and attended to show them solidarity as Mr Lawrence has supported us.

The Macpherson Report, published on 24 February 1999, found the investigation into Stephen's murder was "marred by a combination of professional incompetence, institutional racism and a failure of leadership by senior officers".

Returning to the MacPherson Inquiry, our solicitor made submissions for our case to be included into the second phase of the MacPherson Inquiry, which was the phase when the Inquiry travelled across the country to hear experiences of others affected by racism within the police force. The Inquiry travelled to Greenford and I went there with Suresh, Mon and Balwant. Sir William Macpherson, a retired High Court Judge, and his Panel, which consisted of Dr Richard Stone, Chair of the Jewish Council for Racial Equality, Mr Tom Cook, retired Deputy Chief Constable for West Yorkshire and the Right Reverend Dr John Sentamu, were present to hear from other families or organisations. There was a lot of media presence and most of them were aware of our Campaign.

I recall being angered as I listened to the experiences of other families like mine, and individuals too. I was then told that the panel would not listen to my case as the inquest was still pending even though our solicitors had made a submission for our case to be heard. I recollect standing in the corner talking to Suresh and telling him that if the Panel was not prepared to listen to me, then I would just stand on one of the tables and tell everybody my story. Unknown to me a reporter had heard this and soon my comments spread amongst everyone present. Some journalists who were not happy that I was being prevented from addressing the Inquiry got together as they agreed that I should be given a chance to tell my story. The Panel then retired and when they returned they said I could talk but not give full details of the case due to the inquest into Ricky's death still pending almost two years after his death. I agreed, realising the chance to tell my story always came with restrictions on what I was allowed to say.

I agreed to speak despite the restrictions, and my message was clear, that racism within the police force needed to be eradicated. I recommended that the role of the Family Liaison Officer (FLO) had to be changed because of the damage caused to my children. FLOs were not fully trained in how to treat people, especially young children. I recommended that they should be fully updated about the case before they attended the families to update about the cases and not be used to gather information on the families and report as to who came, what was said, etc. After the Lawrence Inquiry came the inquest into Ricky's death, almost two years after his death. I have addressed this in detail in Chapter 5 and it was a crucial, path altering moment in Ricky's case.

After the inquest, we continued to Campaign for justice, and in fact we have never stopped.

Kingston Council organised five Memorial Lectures for Ricky at Guild Hall in Kingston held on the anniversary of his death. The speakers over those years included Mr Michael Mansfield QC, Mr Imran Khan QC, Mr John McDonnell MP, Dr Richard Stone, Ms Yasmin-Alibhai-Brown.

These lectures were very well attended and helped honour Ricky's memory, reminding us of what we were fighting for. They helped like-minded people meet one another to broaden the fight for justice to support other families and causes. Mr Bruce McDonald understood how important it was to have these lectures in Kingston, the place where Ricky lost his life. I felt that by having these lectures in Kingston Ricky was given peace and respect. It was also to see if anyone could remember what happened in Kingston on 14 October 1997 and would come forward with any information.

This was important because the Campaign and the attempts to seek justice were not isolated to only finding out what had happened to Ricky and why we had been treated so appallingly by the police, but also to support the wider movement for justice for all, and to support other families and individuals who have been murdered or suffered racism at the hands of the police.

Such movements can only be successful with support, and not in isolation. This was clear to me from the time when Ricky went missing, because the police were taken aback. They were not just dealing with a grieving family that they could try to placate or patronise into submission, but also a wave of support from professionals and the public alike.

Bruce McDonald was our contact at Kingston Council. He was a pillar of support and understanding and this remains the case even now that he no longer is in the employ of Kingston

Audience at the memorial lectures in Kingston

Council. He is now a Lib Dem Leader of Elmbridge.

Kingston Upon Thames has a draw for me. It was not

somewhere my family and I had really ever visited before Ricky's death, save for maybe one or two occasions to shop. It was and still is considered a very upmarket, affluent area and today a two-bedroom flat brings in a monthly rent of £2,500 to £3,500! It is home to luxury brands in its luxurious shopping centre, which is flanked by cobbled streets and expensive restaurants. But now, it draws me in because it was the last place Ricky went, it was where his body lay for a week in the freezing Thames; it was where we searched day and night at first for signs of life and then for answers as to how he met his death. Even now I feel Kingston calls me but when I go there I feel empty but my eyes are always searching for Ricky. I can't explain this feeling even though my head tells me he is not here but my heart refuses to let go.

I vividly recall one night when we had been out campaigning, standing near the river where Ricky was found, leaning against the fence and sobbing, oblivious to my surroundings. A young man who appeared to have had a few drinks came to me and asked what he could do to make me stop crying. There were a few more encounters like this.

Mr Richard Stone, who was on that panel, was a Guest Speaker at the 5th Ricky Reel Memorial Lecture at the Guildhall, Kingston on 18 October 2003. He paid a tribute to Ricky and I reproduce here what he said, with his permission, as it speaks of how, in his own experience, the authorities who were supposedly there to help, tried to shut us down:

> *I feel greatly honoured to have been asked to give this 5th Ricky Reel Memorial Lecture in memory of a young man who, from all I have heard and read, was full of promise and love. I am sad to be reminded that the family is now six years since that terrible death, yet they have seen nothing which even begins to feel like justice for him. The Lord Chief Justice recently repeated the obvious truth that "justice delayed is justice denied".*

My son went through a serious illness in 1997. What I dreaded as a parent at that time actually happened to Mr and Mrs Reel. Our son was 24 when Ricky died. He was 21 when Stephen Lawrence was killed. If my family had had to face what the Reel family and the Lawrence family had to cope with, I think that we, like them, would have treated the apologies given by the police with the disdain which has surprised those senior police officers who gave apology after apology. Apologies which are not followed by visible and dramatic changes in the attitudes of the apologisers make the apologies feel empty.

I first met Mrs Reel during the public hearings of the Stephen Lawrence Inquiry. She was one of the faces which were there, scrutinising us every day that we appeared in public. As a matter of courtesy I introduced myself during coffee breaks to most of the people who were regular attenders. I was asked by my colleagues who it was that I was sitting there listening to for so long, and I explained how Mrs Reel was the mother of the Ricky we had read about in the newspapers, and who was convinced that her son had been murdered even though the Kingston Police insisted that it was an accident, and that it was Ricky's own fault that he had died

For understandable reasons Mrs Reel wanted a Lawrence-type inquiry for her son. At the very least she wanted to be able to tell our Inquiry what had happened to her son and the way that the police failed to treat it as a murder.

This caused consternation in the Inquiry. If we were to hear presentations from families in addition to the Lawrences, complaining about inadequacies in police investigations, then we would have to give the relevant police officers an opportunity to give their side of the story. This would mean lawyers to sort out what questions those police officers would be asked and the officers would have to receive "Salmon" letters, that is to be notified in advance of the areas of questioning. We would then have to give ample opportunity to the officers to respond, as well as to give time to the Reel and any other family to tell their stories to us, possibly also offering funding for legal representation. I took it upon myself to explain this to Mrs Reel in the following days and weeks.

It somehow happened, as many of you may know, that Mrs Reel did get an opportunity to be a witness to the Lawrence Inquiry. She was to be a member of the team of the Ealing Monitoring Group, which had been invited to make suggestions to us in public during one of the public meetings we held in six inner city areas in Britain during Part II of the Inquiry.

There was whispered consternation when she was seen sitting next to Suresh Grover. 'We can't have that woman telling us about her son, or we'll be into the whole business of another judicial inquiry into her case. That could take months if not years, and land us with £2m or more of costs'.

'I'm sure she will behave properly,' I responded. 'Mrs Reel isn't someone to put us into that sort of embarrassing situation. I think you'll find that she'll do the proper thing and go no further than make suggestions for Recommendations for the future, based on her personal experience'.

And that is exactly what Mrs Reel did. She was introduced by Suresh Grover, then said [more or less] 'I am Mrs Reel. My son was the victim of a racist murder in 1997, but the police refused to treat it as a murder, saying for far too long that it was an accidental death. From my experience I think that the police need to change in the following ways'. And she went on to make helpful and realistic recommendations, which were taken seriously by the Inquiry.

As we left the building later that day the judge said 'You know these families—they have really suffered deeply from failures of policing'. That sort of comment from a lawyer trained to keep emotions separate from the intellectual approach to legal cases was, in my view, quite a triumph for Mrs Reel. In my view she contributed immensely to the passion which infused the language and the dynamism of the Report of the Stephen Lawrence Inquiry.

I believe that Mr & Mrs Reel and their other children, as well as Doreen and Neville Lawrence, and Duwayne Brooks—none of them have yet been able to reach what you might describe as 'closure' on their suffering as a result of the failure to bring the killers of Ricky, and the killers of Stephen Lawrence to justice. All the drama and the changes which have come out of the Lawrence Inquiry do not feel like justice for what happened to Stephen Lawrence in 1993. Mrs Reel may have been heard briefly by Sir William MacPherson and the three of us Advisers, but she too has no prospect of the killers of her son being brought to justice. If it were my son instead of Stephen Lawrence or Ricky Reel, I know that I too would have such huge anger at what happened to him, and what did not happen in the way of thorough policing, that I too would probably find it impossible ever to find in my heart forgiveness for the murderers, or for the police officers who so badly let me and my family down.

Sometimes I read of families who do seem able to go to

places like the Middle East and meet not just families of other victims of suicide bombings, but parents of suicide bombers themselves. I am not sure that I could bring myself to do that, but I do admire people who are able to make something positive out of such a dreadful business as the brutal death of a son.

The effect on brothers and sisters is a whole other discussion which warrants hours of examination of feelings of loss, as well as a kind of guilt which most adult relatives can hardly begin to fathom. This I find requires a very specialist kind of psychotherapist if the siblings are to come through the experience emotionally capable of future sustained loving relationships.

For Mrs Reel and her family; for the Lawrences; the family of Rolan Adams; the Sylvesters; the McGowans; the Mensons and so many other families, I hope that they will one day reach a point where they can feel a sense of justice, closure and peace of mind. Those positive feelings depend on genuine acknowledgement by others of wrongdoing, coupled with significant changes in practice. The families cannot bring about those changes alone. So it is for all of us who care for them to work out who it is who needs to change, and work out how they can most effectively be brought willingly, or unwillingly to make the change.

It is often assumed that black people have to deal with racism. However, this assumption covers up two kinds of escape from responsibility by white people who don't really believe racism is something they want to address. It is those of us who are not Black who have to change what is in our heads, and in the way we act when in the presence of Black people. So, the institutional racism faced by the Reel family can be complained about—vociferously—by Sukhdev Reel, but the change has to come from white, [mainly] men— like me. Women got the vote in Britain, it was the men in Parliament who had to change the law, even though it was in response to the activism of strong women, who harnessed their anger to effect change, just as Sukhdev Reel has got as far as she has by harnessing her anger. Let's face it, none of us would be here today but for her grit, imagination and determination. Certainly this middle class, middle aged white man would not be here giving a lecture on institutional racism but for the activism of Mrs Reel, Sukhdev Reel, we salute you!

Sukhdev Reel didn't need any definitions to know that police officers most wilfully ignored the possibility that her son had been murdered. She also knew that a large part of the reason for that failure was their prejudice about Asian and Black families. When the apologies came, very much later, for her it was just like it had been for the parents of Stephen Lawrence: a feeling that, whatever definitions of institutional racism you care to write, the collective failures of the police were hugely affected by the reputation and morale of the police, like that of the medical profession, is desperately undermined by exposure of the sorts of failures for which, faced by their inactions and wrong actions in the Reel and Lawrence cases, police have had grovellingly to apologise for again and again.

This leaves me with what police officers should perhaps have done on the night of Ricky Reel's death, which would have resulted in all of us not meeting here tonight.

The police may not have been able to prevent what now seems certainly to have been a murder.

However, I suggest they were justified in reassuring Mrs Reel at first that the most likely cause of late arrival home of a teenager is teenage rebellion.

Where they went wrong was to look no further for a cause. They had heard stories of young Asians rebelling against their traditional background, and they assumed that this was all the incident was about. In short, they had a negative stereotype, which is racist in origin, and this stereotype resulted, as I mentioned earlier my police officer friend had told me would happen, in racist officers being incompetent officers. The police officers on that night should have asked the further questions which seek out the possibilities of something more sinister, just as I as a doctor have to ask questions that might point to appendicitis as the cause of a tummy ache.

Had Ricky been a target of attacks in the past? When told his name was "Lakhvinder Reel, known to his friends as Ricky", they were right to assume he was from an Asian background. But that should not be a signal to exercise their discretion not to bother to take the questions any further. A thoroughly professional, racism-aware police officer would automatically seek out whether there was a history of verbal or physical racism against Ricky, or generally in the area where he had been that night.

I have been told that the local police knew of racists in the area. They could and probably should right away have put out a message to all officers asking for any information about racists or muggers seen acting suspiciously or aggressively in Kingston that evening.

You can probably think of other actions they could have taken. I think I have made it clear how institutional racism probably reduced the professionalism of the police on that dreadful night. Some of it could be due to what the Lawrence Inquiry defined as "unwitting prejudice". Some, sadly I have to admit, would have been perfectly "witting".

Without a deep commitment by white as well as Black people to tackling racism together, seeking and eliminating the racism in ourselves and our institutions; Black families, especially those with a legacy like that of Ricky Reel's, cannot begin to trust their police and the other institutions of the country in which they live. They cannot even trust most people from the dominant community. Nor can they move forward and beyond the dreadful death which haunts them.

I hope my somewhat lengthy analysis, and my stories, will have helped to move Britain some tiny amount forward to a better world for all of us who inhabit these islands

I thank you for inviting me to give this lecture, and for your patience in hearing me out.

During one of the Memorial Lectures a complete stranger (but now a dear friend) Ms Sarah Li, Senior Lecturer at Kingston University who attended one of the lectures, sent me this, again, reproduced with her permission:

Last night I attended the lecture given by the eminent solicitor Khan (now a QC) in memory of Lakhvinder 'Ricky' Reel. Present were the Mayor and Mayoress of Kingston, Michael Mansfield QC, John McDonnell MP for Hayes and Harlington Constituency and Vice Chancellor of Kingston University Peter Scott. The Campaigners for Justice for Ricky Reel and their supporters were also there

After a minute's silence for Ricky the guests were invited to light a candle for Ricky. It was an impressive, moving, serene and dignified gathering, a crowd united, at least that evening, in feeling the family's deep love for Ricky, in being with them and in sharing the sense of deep loss and pain suffered by Ricky's mum Sukhdev and his dad Balwant, not to forget the dignified presence of Ricky's loving brother and his sisters. To Ricky's family the pain of losing such a precious and much-loved son and brother was very raw.

The family, the team of solicitors and the campaigners believed with supported evidence that their dear son whom Ricky's mum called her 'special rose' was murdered by racists.

Last night I heard from Mike Mansfield QC that three years later, the family, their solicitors, the campaigners and supporters have successfully turned the police authority's intended verdict of 'accidental death' around to secure an 'open verdict'. Their success was only achieved after much publicity and struggle with the police authority, the coroner's court and Parliament.

The family and their supporters' commitment to find out exactly how Ricky died has forced a very shy, gentle, quiet, private, family-loving woman and mother to become a determined, courageous campaigner. In her fight against what she and her family regarded as gross injustice, she has to constantly and relentlessly expose herself to unbending, insensitive authorities who just simply did not listen to her, and who had ignored her plea to find her 20-year-old precious and beloved son in the days that followed Ricky's disappearance. She was turned away many times. The family, friends and supporters had to trudge the streets in Kingston. I remember then in 1997 seeing a CCTV of what might have been Ricky and/or his friends walking through a spot in Kingston Town Centre on the evening regional news broadcast

Last night, at first hand, I heard a mother's desperate wish to will her son to get up when she saw him lying in his coffin. Here she was now, standing alone on the platform once again re-living those terrible and painful moments. Her voice was faltering but determined when she read a poem for her dear son. She maintained a dignified composure. Here was a mother whose heart has been broken into a thousand pieces. Here was a loving mother in 'absolute and total pain', yet so determined and strong, for her son's sake. I sense, then, that the hope for justice for Ricky will be realised one day.

I heard Imran Khan addressed his lecture directly to Ricky. He began with 'Dear Ricky, I don't know you but I know of you'. He spoke about Ricky's mum's long struggle with the authority, her despair and pain in finding Ricky no longer in his own bed, his books gathering dust. Her pain of no longer able to hear Ricky call her 'mum', his smiles, his laughter and his zest for life. He spoke about the material and internal loss epitomized by Ricky's untimely death, the loss of dreams for a vibrant young man, full of ambitions for life, but a life so cruelly snatched away

I heard Imran Khan speaking about racism, institutional racism, citing evidence from research statistics in his field. He spoke about the nature of the coroner's court which was supposed to be friendly and compassionate, but instead attempted to discredit the integrity of the family and friends. I heard Imran paying tribute to Mrs Reel, that without her steadfastness, the Campaign would not have come this far, that the road was very long ahead, that the fight for justice must go on, that Ricky would be remembered, that Ricky has ignited the candles and the candles would continue to burn until the day Ricky and his beloved family would get justice. As Imran spoke, I saw last night, the silent weeping of Ricky's mum sitting in the front row, her shoulders heaving up and down. I saw her repeatedly remove her glasses and dry her tears. I saw Ricky's father sitting next to his mum. He was upright and still. I heard a lady who sat behind me sniffing, possibly crying tears of pain she felt for Ricky's mum. I was silent and still, respectfully.

But my proudest moment came when I had the honour of shaking Mr and Mrs Reel's hands, such gentle hands, the hands that had once raised and nurtured their beloved son, held him, rocked him to sleep, touched him, soothed him, cuddled him, hugged him, fed him and caressed him and loved him for 20 years. Such gentle folks, such loss, such pain, such gentle loving parents, such pride. I went to the lecture because I cared about what happened to Ricky, I care about his mum and dad. I care because I am a mother too.

There were many events organised to keep Ricky's case in the public domain and at the same time hoping someone will finally speak and tell us what exactly happened to Ricky on 14 October 1997. A few of these events are as follows:

* 3 February 1998: Press conference with John McDonnell, our MP, in the House of Commons.

* 1 April 1998: Our family, together with Suresh Grover, Mon Matharu and John McDonnell met the Home Minister Mr Alun Michael

* 29 July 1998: Case conference in the House of Commons with Mr Keith Vaz, Mr John McDonnell and Mr Edward Davey.

* 10 September 1998: PCA investigation completed.

* 8 October 1998: Submission given to the Stephen Lawrence Inquiry at Greenford Town Hall.

* 21 October 1998: Supporters of the Campaign ended their three-day hunger strike and then met and appealed to Sir Paul Condon to release the PCA report. For a full three days we did not eat anything and lived mainly on water. After breaking our hunger strike went to Scotland Yard and released 365 white and purple balloons, a balloon for each day of the year we were separated from Ricky.

Demanding Justice for Ricky at New Scotland Yard

* 17 November 1998: Meeting with Home Secretary and request for full disclosure.

* 23 November 1998: A summary of the PCA report received by the family. This document turned out to be just an internal analysis by an officer who was not part of the PCA investigation team. This report was immediately returned to the Metropolitan Police.

* 15 December 1998: The family met the officers from the Racial & Violent Crime Task Force with their solicitor and John McDonnell, MP.

* 15 February 1999: A letter was received from the PCA which stated "the investigation has found there were weaknesses and flaws, the investigation has found your allegations of neglect of duty in respect of (named officers) to be sustained. Sadly, you did not receive from the Metropolitan Police the professional standard of service which you have every right to expect". As we did not agree with the explanation given in the letter, a letter, dated 21 February 1999, was sent to the police by our solicitors, to which we never received a reply.

* 1 March 1999: The PCA Report was eventually given to us and our solicitor under the strict undertaking that we cannot disclose it to anyone else.

* 2 June 1999: During a meeting with the police it became apparent that the police themselves had waived any surviving claim they had that public interest immunity was attached to this document by disclosing it to the other members of the public without our consent. The other persons to whom the Report had been disclosed were members of a "sub advisory group", set up by the Racial and Violent Crimes Task Force at Scotland Yard. Ms Christian, our solicitor, wrote to the Commissioner of the Police requesting that he consent to a withdrawal of the undertaking she and the family had given as to confidentiality since the police themselves had already breached this. She urged him on behalf of our family to publish the Report in accordance with the recommendations of Sir William McPherson. Till this date it had not been made public.

* 8 June 1999: Press conference at the House of Commons regarding the disclosure of the PCA Report.

* 6 July 1999: A meeting with the Home Secretary when the family and supporters once again requested the PCA Report be made public.

* 10 August 1999: A press conference with the police at New Scotland Yard when an appeal, for witnesses was made.

* 1 September 1999: A pre-inquest hearing at Fulham Coroner's court.

* 20 September 1999: Witness statements received from Metropolitan Police solicitors.

With Jeremy Hardy, who spoke often about Ricky's case and travelled with us many times to support the campaign

* 12 October 1999: An appeal for witnesses made on the 'crime watch' programme. The police received six telephone calls.

* 14 October 1999: A torch light procession in Kingston Town Centre to mark the second anniversary of Ricky's disappearance. A candlelight vigil near the River Thames where tributes were paid to Ricky. Mac Rogers sang his Ballad he wrote as a tribute to Ricky. I carried a satin pillow made of purple and yellow flowers (the Campaign colours). At the end of the march we hired a boat and, together with family and friends, laid this pillow in the River Thames in Kingston. Balwant wrote "find the softest pillow God, to rest Ricky's head, give him lots of love,

and one big hug, because my son was the best. His 11 year old brother also wrote a note to Ricky, the brother he looked up to, "a loving memory of a person who loved so much, he cared and shared with everyone he knew, because he was such a loving person, if someone was in pain he helped to ease their tears, because he was such a loving person". All these messages were placed on the pillow hoping he would one day find peace.

* 20 October 1999: An Adjournment Debate in the House of Commons.

* 21 October 1999: To mark the second anniversary of Ricky's death, petitions were handed to the Home Secretary in the House of Commons. Mr John McDonnell MP presented an Early Day Motion asking that the PCA Report be made public. Hundreds of purple balloons were released.

* 23 October 1999: First ever memorial lecture held at Guild Hall in Kingston to commemorate the 2nd anniversary of Ricky's death. The Guest Speaker was Michael Mansfield QC.

* 1 November 1999: An inquest into Ricky's death was reopened at Fulham Town Hall. Michael Mansfield QC represented the family.

* 8 November 1999: The inquest was concluded and the Jury returned "an open verdict".

* 4 February 2000: Follow up meeting with the Metropolitan Police in the presence of our solicitors in London to ascertain what further efforts would be made to investigate Ricky's death in view of the "open" verdict.

* 13 May 2000: 'National Day of Action' demonstration at Scotland Yard London and nationwide. Yellow ribbons were tied throughout Britain in memory of Ricky and to send out

the message that we will not go away.

* 14 June 2000: A meeting with Bedfordshire Police in the presence of our solicitors and John McDonnell at the House of Commons to register a further complaint by the family to the PCA.

* 11 July 2000: Ricky would have been 23 years of age on this day. A tree with a plaque was planted in memory of Ricky by Hounslow Unison at Hounslow Civic Centre.

* 12 August 2000: A bench with a plaque was donated by Hounslow Council and placed by the tree planted earlier in loving memory of Ricky.

* July 2001: A plaque (Always Loved, Always Remembered, Lakhvinder 'Ricky' Reel, 11 July 1977—15 October 1997) was placed in the Guildhall until a Memorial Garden was created for Ricky. In July 2001 this Plaque commemorating my son's life was unveiled at its new home, the Ricky Reel Peace Gardens, at the foot of Kingston Bridge. This was organised by Bruce McDonald. At the Ceremony Mayor Thorn said "for two years this Plaque had its place in the Guildhall, but here it is much more appropriate for two reasons; it is near where Ricky met his death and it is a very public reminder to people of the results of racism". It is still in the same place but changes had to be made last year due to the creation of a cycle lane.

There is a plaque at the entrance of Golden Temple at Amritsar, India, which simply reads "Mr Balwant Singh Reel, in loving memory of Lakhvinder Singh (Ricky) Reel, who left us on 21 October 1997. Age 20. Silent tears still flow". I am a great believer of God and of my faith. I also believe in karma. I hope this faith will one day deliver justice. I went to India in the early days to have this done. To my amazement not only did lots of travellers in the plane recognise me and knew of Ricky's case but also people in India, as this case has been highlighted in the Indian press also. I get messages from all over the world about my Ricky.

* In 1999 Asian Dub Foundation compiled an 11-track CD called "Promise 2 Ricky". Ushma Vyas and Shaista Aziz (now a Labour Party politician), two university students, organised music concerts for Ricky. We met quite a few musicians there including Rishi Rich, who performed for Ricky in Hammersmith.

Backdrop image of Ricky painted by Pritt Kalsi, who has also done so much to publicise the campaign

* In 2020 Rishi Rich, Ameet Chana and Kiranee from Break The Noise Records, together with Raj Ghai (Media Moguls), produced a song named "Justice for Ricky Reel". It is the emotive retelling, through song and spoken word, of my story and the continuous struggle for justice for my son. Again this is my message to the world through music about justice denied. There have been lots of other meetings at various venues. Too many to list.

Addressing public and private meetings was frightening at first but it very soon became the norm. I had to learn many new things and somehow in between I lost myself. My life became split, between life before Ricky, and life after his death.

I did countless televised news, newspaper and radio interviews. When I saw myself on television, I barely recognised myself. Even now when I look back at those pictures, I see a broken-hearted woman who refused to allow the police to break her. I was fortunate in that nearly all of the journalists and reporters I met were good people, who treated me well and reported honestly on Ricky's case. Such was the media interest that I was frequently stopped when out grocery shopping or running errands and asked, "are you Ricky's mum?" or, "are you the mother of that boy in Kingston?". It was strange how people now identified me by reference to Ricky, and to be honest that was probably how I saw myself too. Due to the intense fire burning inside me, I lost myself too, lost my identity, but that anger keeps me alive, the anger asking who killed my son and why gives me energy to continue with my promise I made to my son.

It was truly humbling, to be approached by strangers, who would often console me about Ricky's death and I felt then, as I do now, that people care about injustice, and they show it in different ways. Someone will hold up a placard next to you at a protest or demonstration, some will offer their time to help you print posters, some will hold you up when you are exhausted, some will help you find the words to address a public meeting, some will help you share your story, and others will simply but a hand on your arm and tell you how sorry they are for what you have lost. Each and all of these and all the other countless and different gestures over the years have meant a great deal to me, and never more than on the days that I have struggled to get out of bed, or when I relive Ricky's loss at a meeting or media interview.

The Campaign continues. It will carry on till we get Justice for Ricky, and probably after that to support other families and individuals. Now and then I am asked, "why not move on with your life". It's these very questions that remind me of why the Campaign is so important. Racism has not moved on, in society or within the police. It is alive, it is pervasive and it ruins lives. Till it moves on, I will not and so the Campaign and all it stands for is still here. I live in hope of a time when it is not needed.

Chapter 5

Inquest

So many questions but so few answers this week
Reliving the last moments of your precious life my son
Through the words of others, mostly strangers to you
Those people who took your life, what have they done?

The day arrived that no mother ever thinks she will have to face, even in her darkest moments.

The inquest into Ricky's death was going to be heard. As it loomed, I felt scared and hopeful at the same time. I dreaded hearing the details of Ricky's death being recounted, hearing the post mortem evidence being poured over in graphic detail, and hearing about his last moments.

Simultaneously, I hoped that it would shed light on what had happened to him; that hearing evidence from so many different witnesses might help put the pieces of the puzzle of Ricky's death together. I hoped there might be a "eureka" moment where we would suddenly realise that the cause of Ricky's death had been staring us in the face all along and the anguish of "not knowing" would be over.

As the date for the commencement of the inquest got closer

and closer, the preparation for it began to take its toll.

There were more legal meetings with the lawyers, going back over witness statements, a flurry of correspondence with the police, and, always, that feeling of butterflies in my stomach, that strange mixture of hope and despair.

The inquest was unusual for a variety of reasons. Perhaps one of the most important reasons was there was to be a public inquest, with a jury. Jury inquests are very rare and we had fought hard lobbying for a jury inquest with the support of the Justice for Ricky Reel Campaign and our legal team. We felt strongly that without a jury we would not be accorded a fair hearing.

It turned out to be one of the best decisions we could have made. The police opposed a jury inquest of course, and it was clear to me, from Day 1 of the inquest, that they were upset about it.

It felt like in no time at all, the inquest was upon us just over two years after Ricky's death. I slept even worse than usual the night before. Peaceful sleep had evaded me since Ricky's death but this night was so much worse than normal, filled with disjointed nightmares and fretful waking moments.

I awoke feeling ill and more tired than when I had gone to bed the night before. As always, I knew I had to put one foot in front of the other and I put on my mask to face the world. I mentally, but also physically, braced myself for what might lie ahead. I had been told that it would be messy, it would be traumatic, it would be a roller coaster. But it was more than that. It was a living nightmare.

I recall vividly that my children kept on looking at my face, looking for signs of whether I was coping. I did what I always did; I reassured them that I was okay and told them not to worry about me. My younger daughter was at university at the time, in her first year and was going to meet us there. The entire family was attending except for my youngest son who would have been only 12 at the time. I thought long and hard about whether my elder one, being 22 at the time, should attend the inquest, but in the end both of my daughters told me that there was nothing that would stop them attending because Ricky was their brother. They wanted the answers as much as I did.

The inquest was held on 1 November 1999 at Fulham Town Hall. An inquest is supposed to be an inquisitorial process where the coroner acts as an inquisitor to ascertain "who, when, where and how" someone died. The coroner alone decides which witnesses to call and what issues are relevant.

There was huge media interest in the event and I remember so many radio stations, papers and TV news reporters calling me seeking interviews. Renowned human rights barrister Mr Michael Mansfield, QC represented our family instructed by Louise Christian, our solicitor, and we were supported by our family, the SMG and members of the campaign, not just during the inquest but during the gruelling months of preparation for it too and I can say, with hand on my heart, that without this

Arriving at the Inquest with Mike Mansfield QC

support the outcome of the inquest would undoubtedly not have been so positive.

Before I left home that morning to travel to the inquest on the first day, a well-known reporter came to our house early in the morning and brought me a bouquet of beautiful flowers. I was very touched and pretended in my mind that the flowers were from Ricky, a sign to be strong and press forward, and a way to give myself courage.

During the years leading up to the inquest and the years since, so many of the reporters who reported on Ricky's case have become friends because they treated me like a human being and they treated Ricky's story with dignity and fairness, and we were never made to feel like we were just a "story". It is amazing what a difference that can make to a grieving family seeking justice.

We began the day with a Minute's Silence before the formalities began. The idea was suggested by the SMG and was a beautiful and touching moment. A minute can last a very long time and in that time I silently renewed my promise to Ricky to get justice for him, to be strong for him and be his voice and the voice for others who had or would go through a similar experience.

I asked Ricky to stay by my side again as I had felt then, and still do now, that he is with me. I had never attended an inquest hearing before and nothing can prepare you for it.

On arrival at Fulham Town Hall I was feeling nervous and frightened, but hopeful. The front of the building and the corridors were overcrowded with people, and amongst the crowds my heart lifted when I saw the faces of friends, family and reporters. Within minutes I felt braced and ready to face what lay ahead, because after all, what more could I lose?

I met Mr Mansfield outside Fulham Town Hall. I had met Mr Mansfield many times before the inquest. I am privileged to call him a friend. He must have seen that I was very distressed that day and suggested we take a walk. He, along with others, helped hold our family together during the inquest when many times I felt I could not continue to sit and listen to the evidence given by people.

I entered the room with my family and felt cold and shaky, but I knew I would be strong. I knew I had not come this far only to buckle under the strain. Seeing my extended family reminded me that Ricky lived on in our family and had not been forgotten or lost. It was humbling. We have been fortunate to have a large family that has supported us from day one. My brother Mon attended all the meetings and events from the day Ricky went missing, and he has not left my side since. Any reasonable person, myself included (because I like to think I am reasonable, though no doubt the police would disagree!), would have expected to be able to walk into the courtroom with dignity, peaceably and be allowed undeterred to take my seat and start the hearing. Unfortunately, and like all endeavors that had come before (and since), we were met by hurdles.

We should not have been shocked given the treatment we had suffered so far at the hands of the authorities, but we were shocked.

Shocked, appalled, upset and frankly astonished. I learnt that the police had stopped Mon and Suresh Grover as they entered the building, preventing them from accompanying me into the room where the family were to meet our legal team and some members of the Campaign and commence the inquest.

The police knew without a shadow of doubt that these two were my pillars of support being the two constant figures at each and every meeting with the police. I panicked, no doubt the reaction the police were angling to evoke, and I kept thinking, "What have we done wrong?".

Balwant and I felt like bystanders watching events unfold before us, disconnected somehow, as we were in shock.

My brother is a dignified, quietly spoken man who has barely even had a parking ticket! Imagine losing your child, and then not being allowed the comfort of your own brother's presence during the inquest into your child's death. It was beyond devastating. He was not allowed to attend and witness the proceedings of his nephew's case. Every day he accompanied me to the Inquest but was denied entry to the inquest room together with Suresh. I felt alone, discouraged and had no one with me who could explain anything that I did not understand as Mike was questioning the witnesses. Balwant was sitting there next to me but it was as if he wasn't there. I believe he was having flash backs and he told me later that all he could think during that time was if our son had cried out in pain? I felt like I have been pushed into a room and a door was firmly closed after me. I felt I was being punished, but what was my crime?

He was called as a witness on Wednesday 3 November 1999, the third day. He was denied the ability therefore to hear the evidence of the witnesses that came before him. Suresh and Mon were then told that they would be called later to take the witness stand. They were not given a chance to hear from the witnesses they had found. Mon was the one who accompanied Ricky's friends, the victims of the racial attack to Kingston Police Station, but was not allowed to sit with me to listen to what happened at the police station. It soon became apparent to many that the police had another agenda in preventing Mon and Suresh entering the inquest.

As well as removing my support, the police were trying to suggest that Mon and Suresh had interfered with police work and had intimidated witnesses. None of this was true, but if it had been, pick the first day of the inquest to raise it? The allegations related to a much earlier period after all, far before the inquest?

I remember that the coroner made a comment that he was considering referring both of them to the Director of Public Prosecutions. I fail to understand this action. Mon had been asked by the police to accompany them in a walk round of Kingston, retracing Ricky's steps alongside the boys who had been out with Ricky that night. He had done nothing to interfere with the investigation or to intimidate witnesses, and nor had Suresh, so why the allegations? And the threat of prosecution?

In the end nothing came of the allegations, but it had the effect of intimidating us, and undermining my network of support, on the first day into the inquest into my son's death.

It did mean we also had to quickly get an imminent QC to represent Suresh and Mon on day one to deal with the allegations. We were told that Mon and Suresh were not going to be allowed to come in, all those attempts to rally my courage and strength began to feel wasted as I panicked that I would have to go through the inquest without my brother, and without Suresh.

I saw Mr Benjamin Zephaniah, who was poet in residence at Michael Mansfield QC's chambers, sitting in the front seat of the courtroom gallery wearing one of our "Justice for Ricky Reel" t-shirts. He supported our Campaign. Of his experience of Ricky's inquest, he later wrote, "for some reason unknown to me, the judge in the Ricky Reel inquest asked me to sit next to him. Every now and again he would ask me if I was comfortable, and then he would carry on regardless" (*The Life and Rhymes of Benjamin Zephaniah*, 2018). Benjamin later wrote and dedicated a touchingly beautiful poem to Ricky that still brings tears to my eyes when I read it. It is reproduced here on page 207. Seeing him and others reminded me that I was not alone and I would get through this, just as I had fought to overcome all previous obstacles, and I would not allow anyone to derail all the effort that had gone into preparing for this crucial hearing.

Finally, the inquest commenced, and would go on for six days in total, presided over by the coroner. The room was large, bigger than I expected, and the atmosphere was most certainly charged and oppositional from the moment the hearing commenced.

It was clear that this was not a hearing to establish how Ricky died but rather for the police to attempt to discredit any credible evidence concerning Ricky's death that did not neatly fit into their own theory.

The coroner sat at the far end of the room on a bench raised above the rest of us, facing into the room and facing everyone in the room. The police and their team sat to the far right, our legal team in the middle of the room slightly off to the left and the jury sat to the far left across two or three benches

We sat behind our legal team, my family and I, and above us in a large balcony seating area overhanging where we sat, was the rather large public gallery, which would be filled and spilling over each and every day with the media and members of the public, family and friends.

The hearing proceeded as one would expect, with opening submissions from both parties, and then the hearing of witnesses from the witness box, which was located directly in front of where the police and their legal team was sitting.

Every time a witness was sworn in, I would spend the moments whilst they read off the oath or affirmation, wondering what they were going to say. Would it be simply what was in their statement, would there be any revelations, would they stand up to cross examination. So many of those witnesses who attended to give evidence, when they took the stand, looked at me, not when they started their evidence but usually when they finished it and it was always the same look. It was one of sympathy.

Amongst them were Ricky's GP from birth and his employer—wonderful people who had known Ricky and had impacted Ricky's life. The questions put to me and anyone involved with our Campaign for Justice, made clear to me that the inquest was being used to further the polices' agenda, of trying to suggest that Ricky's death was just an accident, despite the overwhelming evidence to the contrary, and they were trying to discredit the family.

It was apparent to me by the time we got to the inquest that the authorities found us to be a thorn in their side. They had never expected a working-class Asian family, especially a woman, to question them, to challenge their assumptions about Ricky's death, to challenge the racist stereotypes which had poisoned the investigation into his death.

They had never even considered that we might search for our own answers when they failed to investigate. They had assumed that we would accept their sweeping assumptions and the case could be closed, like so many before us. We were not any stronger, any more determined or any more deserving of the truth than any of the other families that had come before us, but we were very lucky to have support from people who were able to help us navigate our way to the truth, and that has made the world of difference.

Most of the questions we were asked during the inquest centered around issues which were nothing at all to do with how Ricky met his death. We were asked why we set up a campaign, when we instructed solicitors, when we made contact with the SMG, why we had spent so much time searching for my son when he was missing and then spent so much time trying to find evidence after we found out he was dead.

It was clear that we as a family, we as a Campaign were on trial for fighting on, when the police expected us to accept what they told us and go away. I recall being asked about Ricky's phobia of open water. The police tried to challenge his fear of open water and questioned his own GP about it. The police had gone through all of Ricky's personal information, his medical records, his university application, diverting so much energy and resources in trying to prove our assertion about the phobia to be not just wrong, but fabricated by us. It was suggested to us that we had made a mistake about Ricky's phobia (having known Ricky his whole life I am not sure how I would have made a mistake about this!) but that we had actually, as a family, made the phobia up.

A question was put to me that Ricky had a love of sports such as running and jogging and liked going swimming so he could not have had a phobia. I answered the question by stating that none of this (Ricky being sporty) had ever been disputed. What I was saying was that he had a fear of open water, i.e. rivers, lakes and the sea. He could go to a swimming pool. Even the most basic assertion of the family, that Ricky had a fear of open water, was still being challenged two years later by the police. It should not have been a contentious point, but as a fear of open water didn't fit with what the police wanted the jury to believe, they challenged it, because if he had a phobia, he could not have gone to the edge of the water and just fallen in accidentally, as the police wanted the jury to believe.

I was also asked by the Coroner about whether I had attended the Stephen Lawrence Inquiry some months earlier (into institutional racism). Again, what relevance had that to how Ricky met his death? The Lawrence Inquiry happened after Ricky died. I attended it to support the cause, and to make oral submissions to it, as many others did too. I have continued to support other campaigns as it is only right that people who have lost a loved one or have been subjected to injustice in any form, need support from others. I feel it is my duty to support people whoever need my support.

I was asked during my evidence to the inquest about what I discussed at the Stephen Lawrence Inquiry, who gave what evidence about Ricky to the Inquiry. I could not understand and still don't understand the relevance of these questions. What was wrong with my attending the Inquiry? Why ask me these questions when lots of other people also attended this event?

During the six days, Ricky's friends who had been out with him the night he disappeared and who were attacked alongside Ricky, gave evidence to the inquest. They were called Dean, Brinder and Maneet. They were young men, the same age as Ricky, who attended the same university as him. It felt strange seeing them after two years, to see how much they had changed in those two years. Their collective evidence described how the intention that night between Ricky and his friends had been to go to a gig at Brunel University Student Union, the same university that Ricky had been attending, which was only about 10 minutes from our home in West London.

Ricky's three friends picked him up in Dean's Mercedes car from our house and they described how their plans had changed after collecting Ricky, with them deciding to go to Kingston town centre instead, to Options nightclub. Kingston-upon-Thames is a very affluent area, but also at the time had a large university and therefore a very active student presence with a number of nightclubs dotted around the perimeter of the well-to-do town centre. On arriving in Kingston, the four of them sat in the car as they were early, having parked up on Down Hall Road. They had alcohol in the car and all four of them were drinking. Ricky drank less as did Dean because he was driving. Brinder was finishing most of Ricky's drinks, we were told.

Ricky rarely drank and when he did he usually drank very little. Sometimes he might have a beer with his Dad at home. It was recalled by his friends that Ricky was his usual quiet self in the car that night. It was also noted, that when he wanted to relieve himself, whilst they were drinking in the car, Ricky had urinated close to the car against a wire fence which fenced off the pavement from derelict buildings just yards from where the car they were in was parked.

Down Hall Road was a street that led from the High Street at one end to the river at the other, and was not very long. On one side it was adjacent to the car park for John Lewis &

CCTV images of Ricky's friends leaving the nightclub after 2am

Bentalls, but with lots of greenery between the road and the car park, and on the other side it was flanked by buildings, some of which were derelict. There was street lighting along it and we would find out later that there was night time building works taking place at the end near the High Street. There were canal boats moored alongside the river at the end of Down Hall Road, where Ricky's body was later found, metres from where the Mercedes car was parked.

Upon leaving the car to make their way across the town centre to the nightclub, Ricky said he had changed his mind and wanted to go home as he was due to attend a meeting in the morning. He was doing a placement year as part of his degree and at that time was working in Central London in IT. It was a Microsoft Conference.

I remember in the days he was missing, searching through the bag that he had packed the night before (always being prepared and responsible) to go to the conference containing his pass, course confirmation, carefully sharpened pencils and two pens in a clear pencil case. How I treasured that bag and its contents in the days following his death.

Brinder and Maneet had their arms around Ricky and we were told that they tried to encourage him to join them in the nightclub but Ricky refused. They were walking and talking and had reached the Bentalls Shopping Centre in Kingston, which was in the middle of the town centre near to bus stops in an area that was largely pedestrianised and reasonably well lit.

The street where the racist attack on Ricky and his friends took place

Ricky was still saying he wanted to go home and said that he would get a bus as there was one which would have brought him straight home.

As they were talking and discussing their plan, with Ricky saying he would go home, two white men shouted "oi Paki" at Ricky and his friends. When Maneet asked them what their problem was, Ricky and his friends were attacked. They were punched and Maneet's turban was pulled at. Brinder tried to intervene to help Maneet and told his friends to "scram" and

Ricky's friends scattered. Maneet ran away and Dean joined him and they ran back towards John Lewis. Brinder ran in another direction towards Bentalls and other shops.

The three boys then got back together again, and they described feeling shaken and scared with painful jaws where they had been punched by the white men. They recalled that they saw two white men running from the direction of the Church, just metres away from where the fight had taken place, and at the same time saw a bus running along Bentalls and John Lewis and they couldn't be sure whether the two white men caught the bus or whether they remained in the area.

Mike Mansfield QC demonstrated that there was some uncertainty about what Ricky's friends reported in terms of the bus they saw. One of his friends originally reported that he thought that the two white men ran towards a single-decker bus, another friend referred to a double-decker bus but it was later established through enquiries that there was in fact no single-decker bus running that night. It was apparent that the friends were not sure whether the two white men got on a bus at all when fleeing the scene, whether they got on a bus or remained in the immediate vicinity of Kingston town centre.

What was clear was that Ricky was never seen alive again after the fight when the friends said that they scattered to get away from the racist attack.

Hearing this evidence from the boys in the witness box was harrowing as it felt as though I was living Ricky's last moments myself. It tore at me in ways that it is very hard to articulate.

It was established during the inquest that a key witness, the bus driver of the bus that was likely to have been in the town centre around the time of the attack, was in fact traced by our family, and not the police, and this was within two days of Ricky going missing. It was established during evidence that the police waited 13 days to interview the bus driver which meant that they didn't interview him at all during the week that Ricky was missing and only after he was found dead. Unfortunately, because of the time lapse, it was established during the inquest that the bus driver's evidence was unclear because by this point it was two weeks after the incident. And therefore the bus driver was not able to recollect clearly what happened that night.

Had the police interviewed him at the time we had passed the details of the driver over to them, the information he would have been able to provide would have been far clearer. He could've been interviewed and should've been interviewed immediately. What was clear was that the bus driver couldn't recollect two white youths running onto his bus.

This was crushing to the police, because their case, that Ricky was unlikely to have been harmed by the two white men, was built on their insistence that there was no evidence that the white men had remained in the area, i.e. that they had gotten on the bus. The police conveniently ignored the fact that the friends did not know if the two white men had gotten on a bus or not and that the bus driver of the bus did not remember two white men jumping onto his bus.

In other words, there was no evidence to suggest the two men had gotten on the bus and left the area, and to suggest therefore that they could not have harmed Ricky.

Ms Hunt, the then investigating officer, also gave evidence to the inquest. Detective Chief Inspector Hunt was appointed to run the Ricky Reel inquiry in November 1998 after I made a complaint about the lack of investigation by the first team (Mr Morgan's Team). When giving her evidence to the inquest, she refused to accept the possibility that the white men may not have got on the bus despite the overwhelming evidence described above.

Why? Because like Ricky's phobia of open water, it simply didn't fit with the police's assumption that Ricky had just accidentally fallen into the river.

Sadly, this demonstrated that the police continued to approach Ricky's death and circumstances surrounding it with a completely closed mind when undertaking their investigations.

Her investigation was flawed in that it failed to consider or investigate the real possibility that the two white men remained in Kingston and therefore may have gone on to harm my son and, having dismissed that as a real possibility, just assuming that Ricky must have fallen into the river.

I still don't know whether it was these two white men who killed Ricky or whether it was someone else in Kingston that night, but what is clear from the evidence is that Ricky's death was not a tragic accident. It became clear during her evidence that Ms Hunt had failed to interview Ricky's friends during her investigation even though they were the last people to see Ricky alive and they were crucial witnesses to the racial attack.

As Ms Hunt's evidence continued, we heard from her and Ricky's friends that, having got back together after the fight, the friends had found one another, and at that point noticed that Ricky was not with them. They said they briefly looked for Ricky but did not find him and assumed that he'd gone home by getting a bus from the town centre. His friends went to Options nightclub till about 2 am.

What was clear from their evidence was that at no point when interviewed when Ricky went missing, or after he was found, were these friends asked whether they recognised either of the two men again.

Devastatingly in the evidence during the inquest, the friends said that if they'd been asked this question, they would've said that they could have recognised the men. This was an opportunity missed by the police.

It was also confirmed, that they were not asked to compile an E fit (an electronic picture of the face of a person being sought by the police, created by a computer program from composite photographs of facial features) or a body map in which they would draw a general outline of somebody with clothing on et cetera.

They were only asked to do a photo fit where they would pick bits of different features and put them together to make an image of their attackers.

They were not shown photographs of suspected racists in the area and in the areas to where the buses from Kingston ran, which should have been done. This would likely have assisted the investigation at an early stage.

During her evidence, Ms Hunt accepted that during the week that Ricky was missing there was no reconstruction of his disappearance to help jog peoples' memories of what they

CCTV images taken in Kingston town centre moments after the attack showing two men in an alley near Down Hall Road

may have witnessed around the time of the attack, which was clearly a police failing and it was a basic investigatory tool in an investigation such as this.

Listening to the evidence of Ms Hunt it was astonishing to find that even two years later the police were still desperately trying to disassociate the racist attack and Ricky's death from one another. Over and over again during evidence the police referred especially to the first week that Ricky was missing as simply a missing persons' investigation, completely dismissing the racial attack, which was not even being investigated as a crime by the police, nor linking it to the fact that he was missing.

Surely if someone is attacked and then is never seen alive again immediately following that attack, especially a racial attack, investigators should treat the events as linked? The police, in my view, simply did not want Ricky's death to have a racist element to it, it was inconvenient for them coming as it did in the wake of the death and public inquiry into the death of Stephen Lawrence and the findings of that Inquiry that determined that the police were institutionally racist.

It was far easier for the police to try and persuade the public through the inquest that Ricky did not die because of a racist attack, but because he slipped into the river accidentally.

On multiple occasions during evidence Ms Hunt referred to the resources that were poured into the investigation into Ricky's death. This was surprising given that at various points of the investigation we were told that certain lines of enquiry (including a reconstruction) had not been undertaken due to limited resources.

We have since found out more than 15 years after the inquest that at the time of this investigation into Ricky's death and at the time of this inquest, the police were actually secretly diverting crucial resources away from Ricky's investigation, instead using them to fund undercover officers to spy on our family. I talk more about this later in the book, as it represents a huge revelation of substantial significance.

It was established during the inquest that there had in fact been a map drawn up of all the CCTV in Kingston, in 1996 (a year before Ricky's death), as part of Operation Rainbow, which was a counter terrorism operation in response to the Docklands bombing. Despite knowing that there was this CCTV map, the police, during the week in which Ricky was missing when CCTV would have been absolutely crucial, failed to consult the map and therefore identify what could have been crucial CCTV evidence in Ricky's case. We learned that despite the map, not all the CCTV that was available was seized and some of the CCTV that was seized, and which clearly would have been crucial to Ricky's last moments (because, for example, it was along the route we know Ricky must have taken immediately after the attack), was destroyed without ever being viewed by the police. It transpired that during the original investigation the police had failed to obtain still images of crucial moments from CCTV that had been seized, including still images of two people, who may well have been the two white men that attacked Ricky and his friends, standing in a dark and narrow passage just off where the attack occurred, timed at just moments after the attack took place.

Throughout her evidence Ms Hunt addressed all of her answers to all questions to the Coroner, who was to her right, and not the jury. All other witnesses had addressed themselves to the jury. At the conclusion of her evidence when Ms Hunt was asked by the Coroner what she thought had happened to Ricky, I recall vividly that she slowly and quite deliberately turned to face the jury and then said clearly that she believed that Ricky's death was just an accident.

I have never seen a more obvious attempt to influence a jury. This concluded her evidence. I was disgusted by her conduct and if I had had a poor relationship with the police before, it was utterly beyond repair now.

Following the inquest, I did make a complaint, which was my second complaint to the Police Complaints Authority (now called the Independent Office For Police Conduct) because although Ms Hunt had assured us when she began the investigation into Ricky's death that she would approach it with an open mind, the evidence that she gave to the inquest showed beyond doubt in my view and in those of most others present at the inquest, that Ms Hunt in fact had not done so. Her investigation seemed to be focused on trying to prove the police's initial and flawed theory, rather than actually investigating what had happened to Ricky. The complaint was taken by Bedfordshire police.

Mr Morgan was the original investigating officer, in effect Ms Hunt's predecessor. He was the one who had interviewed Ricky's friends at the beginning of the case. During the inquest he too gave evidence. It was a truly shocking experience. Reading back over the inquest notes it is shocking to me how many times it was put to Mr Morgan that we as a family had provided him with crucial information from our own attempts to find Ricky and to find out who had caused his death, and Mr Morgan denied it.

He suggested that we had never given him the information, repeatedly saying that we had not brought certain information to his notice. It was clear that we had passed on the information as the police's own records referred to our information during the inquest, thus demonstrating that the police had received the information. Indeed, this was clear from their own records. Mr Mansfield provided the names of police officers who were aware of the messages from us to Mr Morgan, giving important information to him to follow up. It was not followed up. For example, it transpired during his evidence that despite us passing on the details of a crucial riverside witness to the police whilst Ricky was still missing (i.e. within the first seven days), the witness was not in fact interviewed by the police until 16 August 1998, 10 months later!

Astonishingly during his evidence, Mr Morgan tried to suggest that the racial incident and Ricky being missing had been separately reported to the police, suggesting therefore that the family were to blame for the two issues not being investigated properly or together. This was absolutely untrue as the evidence showed that every time we spoke to the police it was in the context of Ricky being attacked and not coming home again. I found it astonishing that the police were still trying to separate out the racial incident and Ricky's disappearance and subsequent death, even two years after his death, and that Mr Morgan seemed to be trying to blame the family for the fact that the police had failed to coordinate the missing persons and racial incident investigations.

Mr Morgan continued to try and assert that the two matters had been reported separately, despite the fact that he accepted the evidence that when the family first contacted the police, we told them about the racial incident immediately.

During his evidence Mr Morgan suggested that the reason he failed to take crucial steps in the investigation at all, or in a timely manner, such as setting up an Incident Room until seven days later, was because he understood that the two white men who attacked Ricky and his friends had gotten on a bus immediately after the attack and left the area.

Was it a coincidence that Ms Hunt had been spouting the same assumption during her evidence? Mr Mansfield had to take him through the statements of Ricky's friends, which demonstrated that in fact none of the three friends were able to say with any degree of certainty whether the two white men had got on a bus and left the area. There was therefore no conclusive evidence that they had left the area at all and it was therefore put to Mr Morgan that clearly the entire premise of his investigation was flawed; he was investigating on his assumption that the two white men had left Kingston when in fact the evidence in no way supported this assumption.

Mr Mansfield referred to the fact that in the report Mr Morgan wrote for the Coroner specifically for the inquest. Mr Morgan had repeatedly referred to the fact that he assumed that the two white men had left vicinity and his investigations had always been based on that assumption. Mr Mansfield successfully demonstrated that in fact this was not at all borne out by the evidence.

It was established that the lack of an incident room during the seven days after Ricky's disappearance meant that there was no proper coordination of the investigation of the racial incident and Ricky's disappearance.

Conflicting and confusing messages were passed to the family. Officers who were supposed to be dealing with the case did not get messages or failed to pass them on—another crucial failing meaning vital evidence was not gathered, preserved or followed up properly.

In fact, many of the witnesses to the facts of Ricky's disappearance gave evidence during the inquest to confirm that they were first approached by my family and supporters and not the police at all or only some significant time later, which demonstrates that much of the investigative work was actually undertaken by our family and if we hadn't found these witnesses they may never have been located.

It was also established during Mr Morgan's evidence that it was my family and supporters who actually seized the first piece of CCTV evidence on 16 October 1997, two days after Ricky's disappearance. We did this by walking the streets, day and night. We did not have the benefit as the police did, of a CCTV map of the area but despite this we found what would turn out to be crucial CCTV evidence showing Ricky in his last moments of life walking past Bentall Shopping Centre, a few metres away from where the fight had occurred shortly after midnight. It was established during the inquest that Mr Morgan's team had failed to seek any CCTV prior to this point.

As I sat and listened to Mr Morgan give his evidence, I was disgusted by his refusal to acknowledge things that had gone wrong whilst he worked on Ricky's case. He refused to take responsibility for anything, and seemed to stick blindly to his "theory" about Ricky's death being accidental, even in the face of overwhelming evidence to the contrary.

One such example is that Mr Morgan was told that a witness, who was in fact a very well-known BBC journalist who had been in the Public Gallery, had passed on a note during the inquest which was about Mr Morgan's approach to the case. The journalist stated that he was present when the river was searched and Ricky's body was recovered (on 21 October 1997, seven days after he went missing). He described that he spoke directly to Mr Morgan no later than 12.35 pm on that day. He said at around 11.30 am he arrived at a stretch of the River Thames near Canbury Gardens. Mr Morgan arrived around 11.55 am and two police officers entered the water and began their search.

Almost immediately Ricky was found floating just beneath the surface a few feet from where the divers had entered the river. He spoke to Mr Morgan a few minutes later and Mr Morgan confirmed that the recovered body was Ricky's. The journalist recorded that Mr Morgan had told him that there was little doubt in Mr Morgan's mind that Ricky had fallen into the river while urinating and drowned and he was not treating Ricky's death as suspicious and did not expect that there would be a criminal investigation into his death.

The journalist said that others had heard Mr Morgan say this. These were the words Mr Morgan had spoken to the journalist when Ricky was found, at the scene of the river recovery, before any post-mortem or forensics from a post-death investigation. It is truly shocking. It demonstrates that Mr Morgan was not interested in finding out the truth of what happened to Ricky.

Mr Morgan's response to this was that he didn't know the journalist and he wasn't aware of the conversation, and this to me represents yet again a further refusal to accept responsibility for his actions and assumptions and to instead blame others, in this case the journalist, at other times the family.

It has to be remembered that a police officer from the same police force had assumed when Ricky was missing that Ricky had probably just run off with a girlfriend or a boyfriend or from the prospect of an arranged marriage which he believed to be common in Asian families.

Mr Morgan is the officer who was officially found by the Police Complaints Authority to have conducted an extremely flawed investigation. He tendered his resignation from the police service in December 1998. Disciplinary proceedings were pending at that time as a result of issues arising from the Surrey Police PCA Report into his flawed investigation into Ricky's disappearance and death. In February 1999 he received an admonishment in respect of this matter and resigned from the Met Police in 1999.

The fact that he felt bitter towards my family and I because of this was absolutely clear, in my view, from the way he gave his evidence during the inquest and his actions toward our family after the inquest, which I will describe later and are hard to believe. Mr Mansfield put to Mr Morgan during evidence all the reasons why yet another of Mr Morgan's assumptions, that Ricky had tried to urinate by the river and fallen in, was flawed.

Mr Mansfield reminded Mr Morgan that Ricky had a phobia of open water, that Ricky and his friends had been using a place to urinate by their parked car by a derelict building so it was quite clear that he knew that he could go quite safely there without endangering his life by going to the river, that there were in fact plenty of places where he could urinate without going to the river and that to go to the river to urinate meant he would have to pass a number of more convenient places to urinate, walk past a car park and pass a barrier through a narrow gap to get to the river.

Mr Morgan was reminded of the fact that Ricky was a very shy person, and indeed everyone who knew him had attested to this fact, so Mr Mansfield challenged Mr Morgan as to why therefore he would assume (without any evidence) that Ricky would go to the edge of the river and face the river, where there is a light and big warning sign and occupied houseboats, and try to urinate in front of everyone.

Even leaving aside his phobia of open water, going to the river to urinate would have been a hugely unnecessarily circuitous thing to do. Mr Morgan was reminded of the fact that the pathologist who had conducted a post-mortem on Ricky's body had said that just because Ricky was found by the edge of the river, did not mean that that was where he had entered the water.

None of the people living on houseboats on that stretch of the water or living next to the riverbank remembered hearing anybody entering the water at that time of night. Mr Mansfield, who visited the site, noted that the edge of the river where his body was found (close to the bank in about four feet of water) was sturdy and strong, not crumbly and weak.

Mr Mansfield pointed out to Mr Morgan that under his leadership, the police had failed to commission any forensic report of the riverbank where Mr Morgan appeared to be assuming that Ricky had slipped and fallen in. This seems hardly surprising given the comments made by Mr Morgan to the BBC journalist at the scene of Ricky's recovery from the River. Mr Morgan's first assumption was that Ricky entered the river close to where his body was recovered.

But the pathologists who looked at this indicated they were not in position to say where he entered the water. What they were able to say was that he would sink at the point at which he drowned, which was quite different.

It was put to Mr Morgan in evidence that when the people in the houseboats moored where Ricky was found were interviewed, they had said that they are used to seeing floating and drifting bodies fished out. Ricky's body was not floating but had been recovered, which was a big difference. These people living in the boats said that they were light sleepers and on that particular night did not hear anything from that side of the river. This suggested that Ricky may have entered the river somewhere else.

In the face of this evidence, you would have assumed that Mr Morgan would have had to concede that his assumption about Ricky urinating and falling in accidentally had to be flawed, surely? But no, his response was to claim that he was unaware that two pathologists and specialists who had visited the site said that they could not confirm whether Ricky had entered the water where Mr Morgan had assumed he did.

Another reason Mr Morgan seemed to assume that Ricky had simply fallen into the river and drowned was the fact that when he was found we were told that the fly buttons on his jeans were open. Ricky had been wearing a pair of jeans that had a few fly buttons on, as was the fashion at the time. Mr Mansfield pointed out to Mr Morgan that he had failed to take into account that many bodies when they are recovered from the water are found with their buttons open because they are loosened by the water and because of the pressure that builds up within the body, as was found to be the case in many of the tragic victims of the Marchioness tragedy.

Mr Morgan clearly took exception to being questioned. I can see why—as the result was to show what we already knew: that his investigation had been critically flawed from the beginning. In my opinion it was racist, and dangerously deficient as a result. He was clearly a man not used to being questioned, let alone by a woman, and an Indian woman at that!

Beyond his evidence, the inquest continued. The police's questioning of my family and our supporters effectively put us on trial.

My own brother gave evidence to the inquest of Ricky's phobia of open water, but the police simply did not accept any such phobia existed despite evidence from his uncle. My brother Mon has been instrumental in our fight for justice. He was there from the moment I called him to say Ricky had not come home, he was with me when I went to the police stations to make our initial reports, when we met with the police, when we undertook searches, at the funeral. He went with Ricky's friends on the 15 October, the morning that he didn't arrive home, to see where they had parked the car and to retrace their steps. He visited Kingston with us every day from that day until the day Ricky's body was discovered. He gave valuable evidence to the inquest. This could not have been easy, given how close he was to Ricky, and all of my children. Mon is very close to me and we live near each other. Our children are of the same ages and our families spent a great deal of time together. Mon was quite harassed at the inquest.

The police had to be reminded once again of the rules of the inquest, and how to appropriately question a witness, and had to be reminded that this was an inquest and not a criminal trial.

During his evidence Mon talked about how we reported the racist attack immediately alongside Ricky's disappearance, how we spent hours on the streets looking for Ricky, about

Ricky's phobia of open water (over which he was extensively cross examined). He was able to explain how there were so many places Ricky could have urinated more privately and more conveniently before he would have even reached the edge of the river. He was the one who had retraced Ricky's last known steps with his friends, and where they had been parked, where they went to urinate etc.

During his evidence, Mon, who is also Chairman of the Justice for Ricky Reel Campaign, was treated as though he was a defendant in a criminal trial, rather than someone assisting the Corner with ascertaining a cause of death. It was harrowing to witness and I recall feeling guilty that he was in this position, because of my campaign, and helpless to do anything to help him.

The lesson was clear however: if you challenge the police— you make an enemy of them.

They questioned him appallingly. In preparation for his evidence the police had assembled a team of approximately 8 to 10 personnel from the Metropolitan Police Service to sit behind their barrister, and they were constantly writing notes and passing these to Ms Hunt and she was also making her own notes and passing them back and forth. Some notes were passed to Counsel for the police. It was obvious that the notes passed to the police's barrister were prompting him to question Mon repeatedly over the same topics. This was despite the fact that he had answered the questions the first time and had provided all the information that he could. It was plainly obvious to all those present at the inquest on that day that the line of questioning being adopted by police Counsel was used as an opportunity to "dirty" the Justice for Ricky Reel Campaign and to implicate The Monitoring Group, and in particular Mr Suresh Grover, in allegations of intimidation of witnesses, which were untrue and for which there was not a shred of evidence.

During the inquest Mon was accused of interfering with police work (because we as a family dared to undertake our own investigation) and he found these allegations extremely distasteful, offensive and without any basis whatsoever. Mon firmly believed that if Ms Hunt had not passed the notes to the Counsel the line of questioning would certainly have followed a different route and it would not have strayed from the business in hand. Many times Mr Mansfield had to stop the evidence to remind the police that the family were not on trial, that this was an inquest.

Ricky's employer was also called as a witness to the inquest. Ricky worked with him in Vauxhall on a one-year placement during his degree. At the time, this was called a "sandwich" course. He said Ricky went to work every day, except for one week when he was sent on a training course. Ricky was due to go to Docklands the next day (the day he did not return home) as it was the Microsoft Launch of Windows 98. Ricky was looking forward to attending this event. His employer said he pushed hard within the company to get Ricky some external training, which was unusual but Ricky was talented. He didn't think the Manager or anyone else in the management of the company was prepared to pay for training, but they made an exception in Ricky's case because he felt Ricky needed some variety. Ricky received a gruelling two-months training. The project was described as "at the cutting edge of internet research and development" and was partly funded by the then European Economic Community. He said Ricky's work was better quality than he had expected. Ricky was almost a bit coy about it when he was asked to show it but his employer was always impressed by what he saw. It was obvious it was a hobby as well as a job to Ricky: that was one of things that impressed his employer at his job interview.

It was quite clear that the police did not believe me about Ricky's work record and that they had created their own profile of my son, which was completely wrong and based on racial stereotypes. In other words, it was entirely based on race, assuming he must be fleeing an arranged marriage or running off with a partner.

The more I listened to the evidence from the police, from

Mr Morgan and Ms Hunt, the more it then made me realise that, as they never accepted that there was a racial attack leading to Ricky's death, I was not surprised they never found Ricky's killers as they never believed they existed! Just months before Ricky's death, close to where I live, there had been a deplorable attack by Asian youths on a young white boy who happened to be a police officer's son. Police had moved heaven and earth to catch the assailants, and fortunately, within days they were found and charged and eventually prosecuted. Not a day goes by when I don't ask why my son's attack, disappearance and death was not treated in the same way?

In addition to witnesses of fact, the police and us, there was expert medical evidence from pathologists who had conducted post-mortems on Ricky. My poor son underwent multiple post-mortems to try and get to the truth of what happened. Even thinking about what he was subjected to in death breaks my heart all over again. My poor beautiful boy.

Ricky was wearing a new shirt on that day when he went out. He had purchased it from River Island. I remember Ricky's sister teasing him about finally discovering what "fashion" was! I showed the receipt to the police. The police returned Ricky's clothing to me on 22 October 1997, the day after he was found, without undertaking any forensic analysis of it whatsoever, which again, given Mr Morgan's comments by the riverside to the journalist, now does not surprise me.

There was no forensic analysis of the area where his body was found, nor of his clothes or personal belongings that were found with his body. The police took them back from me on 18 December 1997 because I pointed out a tear in the shirt. They have never been returned. I have no idea where they are now.

Dr Snow undertook the first post-mortem I believe the day of or the day after Ricky's body was found. He was instructed by the police. Dr Snow stated that he noted two areas of deep bruising underneath the skin on Ricky's back but no surface injury to the skin. He said these bruises were caused before or at the time of death rather than after death. He said it was a possibility that the "deep bruising" injuries to Ricky's back were muscular injuries "caused by violent twisting" because there were no marks on the skin to suggest that a blow had been struck through it". He confirmed that a broad spectrum of blood and urine tests were performed. The analysis for drugs was negative. Alcohol was detected but the results must be considered with great circumspection since the alcohol may either be produced or metabolised after death. Dr Snow said he could neither confirm with certainty nor refute the possibility that Ricky was under the influence of alcohol at the time of his death. Ricky, 20, was a fit young man with no evidence of natural disease that could have caused or contributed to his death.

A buoy marks the spot on the River Thames where Ricky's body was found.

I recall the patronising way Mr Morgan explained the theory to us on the day his body was found, citing his open fly buttons as the main reason. We as a family took the heartbreaking but necessary decision to instruct an independent pathologist to undertake a second post-mortem days later. Dr Peters stated that there were a series of injuries on Ricky's body, near his shoulders (where we had found the rip in his shirt), on his back, near his ribs towards the side of the body. Some were beneath the skin and some were on the surface. The pathologist confirmed that all these injuries were peri mortem, occurring near the time of death. He also told the court that there was no pathological evidence to identify the direction in which Ricky was facing when he entered the water and no significance should be placed on the fly buttons being undone. There could be various reasons. Instead of taking his expert evidence on board, he was cross examined over how many possibilities about Ricky's death our family gave him when he was instructed, who instructed him exactly, when did he speak to us, and where and who was present at this meeting?

The police then instructed a third pathologist, Dr Right, to undertake a third post-mortem of poor Ricky. This pathologist said that he had not actually examined Ricky himself but had prepared his report having surveyed photographs and reports. He was asked about his opinion on whether the injuries happened before death or if they were the result of falling into the water. He said that some of the blunt trauma injuries could have occurred before entering the water, which was significant. He also agreed that the injuries, if they occurred before entering the water, could be the result of an assault. He added that one could not exclude the possibility of an assault and confirmed that if somebody is standing at the edge of the river and was pushed, there would be no injuries at all.

The police cross examined the third pathologist asking whether due to Ricky drinking it could have been the case that Ricky was unsteady on his feet and could have fallen in accidentally. Mr Mansfield asked Dr Right if he was aware of any witness with Ricky on the night who had suggested that he was unsteady on his feet. He said he did not know anyone who had said Ricky was unsteady on his feet, and that is because no one had suggested Ricky was unsteady on his feet. Mr Mansfield pointed out that in the CCTV clip of Ricky walking along a pavement immediately after the attack, he was walking normally and was not unsteady on his feet. Dr Right said he was not made aware of this video.

There was then a fourth pathologist, Mr White, who again did not examine Ricky. He said that he was asked by the police to review the reports of all the other pathologists together, obviously with some background information and the photographs. He stated that there was bruising over the spinus processes in the middle of the back, and that one sees these types towards the lower part of the back. He said these types of injuries would occur due to a fall from quite a height! He said that one could not get these types of injuries from falling from a normal riverbank, but the injury on the back and the right chest occurs when somebody tears some muscle fibres as a result of trying to extract themselves from a dangerous and a difficult situation.

He also said that the injuries to Ricky's back could well have occurred before he entered the water. Whether they arose from falling from a large height or from before he entered the water, he was quite clear that the injuries did not arise by falling into water from a distance of four feet, which was the distance of the drop from the bank to the water where Mr Morgan had assumed Ricky had entered the water. He said he had not seen Ricky's clothing nor had he seen any report in relation to these!

I almost collapsed in court again when the post-mortem report was discussed. I could not bear to see and hear what was done to my son during each post-mortem. I could not breathe and joined my brother and Suresh outside the hall for a few minutes. All the pathologists accepted that it was not possible to rule out third-party involvement and agreed that there could be a number of explanations for the buttons being undone. I was told that the existence of the shirt damage and the shoulder injury at the first post-mortem remained unresolved with the result that their potential relevance to the events of 14/15 October 1997 could not now be resolved (as the police had failed to forensically analyse the clothing).

During evidence, the Campaign came in for heavy criticism by the police for other reasons too. We were told by the police that they had calculated that we had spent almost 12 or more hours every day in Kingston looking for Ricky during the week he was missing.

I found it very uncomfortable to learn that the police had not only calculated this but also presented this information to us in an accusatory way, as if we had done something wrong by searching for our son ourselves. Of course, we now know that the police were actually secretly spying on us (see my later Chapter on this) when they were supposed to be investigating this case, so looking back now, their comments are not surprising, but at the time it was disturbing. Any parent whose child is missing will move heaven and earth to find them, and we were no exception, but the police had clearly taken exception to our actions. If we had not done this, much of the evidence that we do have would never have been found.

Mr Morgan gave evidence that he had invited media to the river search for Ricky's body on 21 October 1997 to try and generate media interest as he claimed (I would say incorrectly) that there had not been much media interest in Ricky's case. Yet Ms Hunt in her evidence said that the Campaign had talked to the media so much and as a result the two white men shown in the CCTV had been branded "racist murderers" and they would not come forward. This is an example of one police officer from the Metropolitan Police contradicting another and criticising the family and Campaign, yet again, for enlisting help from the media when it was clear the police could not do their job properly!

There was what we felt was an endless stream of witnesses. Every day I left that courtroom feeling broken, every night I relived what I heard during the day and every morning I tried to piece myself back together. I had to be strong, for my children, for my husband. My husband was in pieces too. He was trying to be strong for us all the time. He was broken, but didn't want to show it. Even now, when he sees something on the news about a child going missing or, worse still, dying, he sobs, chest heaving silent cries of pain. We both do. He has a picture of Ricky by his bedside. I too have one next to my bedside and over my mirror. There is a huge painting of Ricky commissioned by my daughter in law and son, hanging above our sofa in the living room. It was a beautiful thoughtful gift commissioned for us a few years ago. In their own way, my children are also showing how much they miss Ricky. The picture of Ricky used at his funeral, that leant next to his coffin, hangs near my husband's bed. In each and every one of those pictures he is smiling back at us, and sometimes when I am at my lowest, I smile back at him and this helps me dry my tears.

Finally, the last witnesses gave their evidence to the inquest. The barristers gave their closing submissions and closed their cases and the jury went out to deliberate. In no time at all the jury returned, and instead of delivering an "accidental death" verdict, as I believe the police had hoped, the jury delivered an "open" verdict. The police were visibly shocked. They clearly had not expected to fail in obtaining an accidental death. I too was shocked. I had been so used to the police getting their way that I could not believe that finally, f-i-n-a-l-l-y, our voices had been heard. I have no doubt that if we had not had a jury to fairly and objectively weigh up the evidence, the result would have been quite different. I remain grateful to the jury for giving me my first glimpse of justice along this difficult road finding out what happened to my son. And I hope if any of them reads this, they come to know how they changed my life that day.

My relief following the verdict, however, was to be short lived. I have discussed at some length Mr Morgan's involvement in Ricky's case. I have explained how his baseless and, in my view, racist assumptions prejudiced beyond repair the investigation into Ricky's death. I've told you that he was recommended for disciplinary action for his failings, but as is so often the case, he simply retired before he could be disciplined. You'd think that after the inquest, given his retirement from the Metropolitan Police some months earlier, his involvement with my family would have come to a natural end. But you would be wrong.

In March 2001 I was at home in my bedroom lying down because I was ill. My phone rang and I answered it. Since

Ricky's death I always answer it because, I think, at the back of my mind I am always hoping that the next call will be the call that tells me who killed Ricky. It was a reporter, Ms K, from a national, well-known newspaper. Something in her voice made me shudder as she seemed hesitant to say what she was

Socialist Worker report on the jury's verdict at the Inquest

calling about, which was immediately suspicious. She asked me if I knew that Mr Morgan had taken with him when he retired from the Met Police Force, graphic photographs of Ricky's body taken during the post-mortem as well as other documents. I don't know how I managed to get my words out but I did and I said that it was not possible because he had retired and the documents and photographs did not belong to him as these were property of the Metropolitan Police. She then asked if I had seen the photographs of the post-mortem. I told her I had never seen the photographs as I was unable to bring myself to view them. I wanted to remember Ricky as he was. I cannot see these distressing photographs. When asked why she was asking me these questions, she then told me that she had had a four-hour meeting with Mr Morgan where he had shown her those photographs and wanted an article printed in the paper with these photographs to tell "his side of the story".

She must have heard or felt my distress as I felt hesitance in her voice as well. I quickly ended the call and opened my bedroom window and tried to jump out. I could barely breathe, think, or do anything. I thought that was the last straw. All I could think of was why did he want these photographs printed in the paper for the whole world to view? Was it some sort of grudge? Why did he want the world to see my son in that state? What did he hope to achieve to strip my son of his dignity in front of the whole world? Why had he taken the evidence into his retirement with him? I was not responsible for the loss of his employment. I had never meant to hurt or harm anyone; just like any other mother, I just wanted a proper investigation into Ricky's death. I need to know how and why my son died and I long for peace.

In desperation I contacted Suresh, who then contacted my solicitor on my behalf. My Solicitor wrote a letter on 14 March, 2001 to the then Director of Public Prosecutions. A copy of my solicitor's letter was also sent to the House of Commons. Mr Sadiq Khan, my then solicitor (now the London Mayor), spoke to the journalist on 14 March, 2001, who confirmed that she met Mr Morgan for four hours. During the course of the meeting Mr Morgan mentioned that he had instructed a pathologist to remove the skin from Ricky's body and that he had photographs in his possession of this post-mortem. It was understood from Ms K that she was shown photographs of this by Mr Morgan.

At that stage we were unaware of what further documents, statements and other matters Mr Morgan still had in his possession. We asked them to urgently investigate whether Mr Morgan had committed any criminal offences in relation to the above matter. We were particularly concerned by the fact that Mr Morgan had police property relating to Ricky's case belonging to the police in his possession and in relation to the timing of any unauthorised post-mortem he might have instructed a pathologist to carry out. We at no stage gave Mr Morgan permission to carry out a further post-mortem. Nor did we give permission for the removal of skin from Ricky's body. We were told by the police that no organs had been removed from Ricky's body; but the skin is the largest organ of the body with a total area of about 20 square feet. And so, this was another assurance by the police that turned out to be false.

We couldn't understand what was going on and felt once again we were let down. I thought I had lost my senses and I was screaming, please let my son have some peace, let him have rest, do not destroy his memories or strip away his dignity. He was not there to protect himself. Nobody heard these screams, nobody saw my tears which I was unable to control and these tears even to this day continue to fall. So hurt and angry we asked questions:

a. *I wanted to know that during the investigation by Surrey Constabulary, why were these photographs left in Mr Morgan's possession?*

b. *During the further investigation conducted by Bedfordshire Constabulary, why were these photographs still in Mr Morgan's possession and not retrieved?*

c. *Bearing in mind that these photographs had been left in Mr Morgan's possession for whatever reasons, it did not give him any right to make these photographs available to third parties in support of his own resignation or the role played by the Metropolitan Police.*

d. *I needed to know who authorised Mr Morgan to use and retain these photographs after his retirement?*

e. *Having been a police officer for over 30 years, surely*

he should have known that this evidence should not have stayed in his possession following retirement from the Met. I was also keen to know whether the (2nd) New Chief Investigating Officer, Ms Hunt, was aware of the above.

I received a reply from the Home Office, Charles Clarke MP, that the investigation of crime, or alleged crime, is the operational responsibility of the police and that Ministers have no powers to intervene in this. I was advised to contact the Commissioner of Police for the Metropolis as well as the Director of Public Prosecutions (who we had already contacted).

The police tried to contact the reporter, who told them to submit a list of questions in writing to the editor. She said she was not prepared to meet the police but would prepare a written response. The editor later told the police that the reporter would not be made available for an interview or to answer questions. They claimed journalistic privilege.

On 23 October 2001 I received a letter from the Chair of the Metropolitan Police Authority. It advised that after taking legal advice from the paper, Ms K had refused to be interviewed. A search warrant to search Mr Morgan's house was not possible due to the lack of cooperation from the paper. But the police officers visited Mr Morgan's home and interviewed him under caution. I was told that due to non-cooperation from the reporter the evidence of others would be hearsay. Mr Morgan handed over the photographs when interviewed. He also said he had no other property in his possession other than reports he had produced himself and those obtained by his MP. He declined to show these to the officers stating they were not the Met's property. I was told that the officers who interviewed Mr Morgan had no authority to search for or demand this documentation.

The CPS informed me that no criminal offence had been committed by the officer, even though he had in his possession property of the police and had disclosed it to a third party and the police had proof of this. Since the police and CPS work closely together I fail to understand how such sensitive police information can be kept in a civilian's home, and the CPS were content to turn a blind eye. No wonder so many cases are overlooked by them. I am told that most complaints about the police are investigated by the officers own professional standards department, which has no vested interest in upholding complaints against its own members. As a result, the complainant is usually informed there is no case to answer, or a process to discredit the complainant occurs to support the officer in question. Once again, we had a situation where we are victims of deeds without any remedies.

I had always wondered why Ricky's body was in such an unbelievably bad state at his funeral. When we saw his body for the first time—he was at the Chapel of Rest and he was cold but he looked like Ricky, like my son. We visited him at the Funeral home and he still looked like Ricky. You couldn't see all the many scars from the post-mortems—his face still looked like him. We decided to have an open casket funeral so all those who loved him could say goodbye. On the day of his funeral, when the coffin came home and the lid was removed, my family was very distressed. My daughter, who had been strong all the time and had promised to stay by Ricky's side throughout the funeral as her last chance to be with her brother, screamed and would not go near her brother again. We had no choice but to keep his coffin closed. His body, including his face, had deteriorated to the point he was barely recognizable. We never understood why, until then, when we found out that Mr Morgan had singlehandedly, without our permission or knowledge, authorised a further post-mortem and the removal of all of this skin. Can someone please tell me why? I still have nightmares about this. I am lucky if I get 2 to 4 hours sleep at night because what my son experienced when he met his death and by his subsequent treatment by the police both in terms of his body and his case still haunts me. No mother would put her child under this nightmare. My mind asks what if this article had gone in the national newspaper? I don't think our family would have survived the publication. And I hate to think what these pictures would have done to my already traumatised children. The law that is supposed to protect let us down again and again.

VERDICT 13.11.99.
I stood on the cold steps holding my breath
The big brown doors were opened wide
To reveal the make-believe courtroom
Where my son's fate would be judged inside

Soon it filled with people
A sea of faces in the gallery
My life for those 6 days Seemed to be
lived on a different plane of reality

The whole hearing seemed unreal
Just actors playing their parts accordingly
And I felt no more than another actor
As the performance unfolded before me

I came with a heart full of anticipation and hope
The thought of getting justice gave me joy
But my heart froze as my son's dignity
Was thrown around the courtroom like a broken toy

My legs longed to stand up in indignation
My lips ached to protest
My arms cried to protect my son
And hug him close to my chest

Had he not suffered enough yet
Why in their lies did they persist?
A chance to try and wear us down
The authorities could not resist

As they told lies, read the distressing details
My heart broke again and again
How I longed to protect your memory sweetheart
As I drowned rapidly in the pain

Your name was mentioned with such a casual air
In that room every minute of the day
As if the person behind the name, like your dignity
Had been steadily chiseled away

Your name so precious to me
Bound up with so many memories
Mentioned by those who did you wrong
Made the tears in my eyes freeze

Those who should have found your killers
Sat before me telling lie after infinite lie
Though I wished to stand and shout out the truth
I could do nothing but sit quietly by

I sat in the dock before the court
And answered the endless questions posed
And your face, urging me on I saw
Each time my eyes were closed

Each word I heard, each witness I saw
Reaffirmed the dreaded fact
That my darling son was gone forever
Never to come back into my arms again

I can only try to describe my sadness
But my words always fail me
They cannot accumulate
The pain the world cannot see

The times I wanted to cry out

Inquest

Wasn't it enough my son was dead
Without them eroding his dignity
With each evil lie that they said

I fooled myself when I thought my son was free from pain
Before me his dignity and privacy was ripped to shreds
By the hearing which was supposed to find out how he
died
Turned into a political battle instead

Six days and five nights I spent in hell
Waiting, wondering at my fate
Why am I alive today
Why my heart is not full hate

The moments before the verdict
Seemed infinity more like years
And when the verdict was read
I failed to hear it through my tears

The shouts and screams around me
Told me some justice had been given to my son
The two years of exhausting battle
Had now this moment been partly won

Darling Ricky this victory is yours
But my fight does not end here
Not till I have got you justice
Though it may take year after painful year

Sweet, sweet son of mine Ricky
With each beat of this mother's aching heart
I remember your face as I laid you to rest
And so remember the promise of justice I set out from
the start
RIP

Chapter 6

Police spying

Look over your shoulder, look out of your window
Prying eyes wait there to find you
Just when you think you have borne the final insult
You will find that they can still hurt you

The Campaign meetings continued as no one involved in the Campaign had given up. Ricky's loss was still fresh and painful, but sometimes, against your will, life has a way of pushing you forward toward joyous family milestones. I felt joy at university graduations, marriages, grandchildren, and more. Alongside our joyousness someone was always missing from these events. Ricky was always missed. Always mourned. Out of the blue, Suresh received a letter from the police of the Operation Herne Team, dated 3 July 2014.

The Undercover Policing Inquiry is looking at undercover policing in England and Wales from 1968 until 2008.[2] Officers were recruited from London's Metropolitan Police Service Special Branch to target individuals and political groups around the country. This of course is the SDS (Special Demonstration Squad). It was superseded by the NPOIU (National Public Order

Intelligence Unit), which had its genesis in about 1986-1999 and continued into the 2000s.[3]

Given false identities, many officers lived double lives, having sexual relationships and children with political activists while continuing to live with their own families. This has become known as the "spy-cops scandal", currently under investigation as the Undercover Policing Inquiry by Sir John Mitting. He was appointed as the Inquiry's Chair in 2017. Before that the Chair was Sir Christopher Pitchford, who stepped down due to ill health. Covert techniques are those used to gather information about a person who is unaware that such an attempt is taking place. This covert techniques in many instances appears to breach citizens' rights under the European Convention on Human Rights (which is directly part of UK law by virtue of the Human Rights Act 1998, but to which the UK signed up in the 1950s). Relevant rights include respect for private and family life (article 8), freedom of expression (article 10) and assembly (article 11). For me and my family, and others who are grieving the death of a loved one, and are concerned about the State's role in the death or the deficiencies of the police investigation and/or inquest, the key right is the right to life (article 2).

Operation Herne is the title given to the investigation led by Derbyshire's Chief Constable Mick Creedon QMP into the Special Demonstration Squad (SDS). The SDS was a covert unit of the Metropolitan Police Special Branch (MPSB). Operation Herne's terms of reference were to review the former SDS from its origin in 1968 to its closure in 2008, examining how it operated throughout its existence.

The letter advised that the police had some information they wished to discuss with our family or legal representatives before 24 July, 2014 as these findings were going to be released to the media on that day. I thought maybe some new leads had been found in Ricky's case and agreed to meet them in John's office. Also in John's presence would be Suresh, Mon and my daughter.

When the day of this meeting came my husband was unwell

so I told him to stay at home. Everything was getting on top of him. This felt like another blow seeing how desperately he wanted to know how Ricky died. He pretended to be strong but I could see the tears he thought he had hidden.

Any sad news on TV still upsets him, especially if it is about a young person but despite despondence, Balwant always put our family first, especially our children, knowing I was unable to be with them most of the time.

I was leaning on him for support. He had picked me up many times. I had fallen with grief and sheer exhaustion, times I had forgotten to eat and when I was unable to carry on past the pain associated with trauma. He had taken me to hospital when I nearly died. He was also feeling these emotions. He was demoralised and upset, yet somehow managed to look after all of us.

He would go to the garage, lock the door and come out after a few minutes. His eyes and face told me that he had been crying. He needed a break. The poor police investigation into Ricky's case hurt him badly; we were no nearer the truth about our son's death. He did not want me undergoing more stress, but he understood my commitment to this cause. So I went to the meeting without him.

Remembering the day of the meeting with officers from Operation Herne Team plays on my mind and leaves me angry. The officers informed us that the Justice for Ricky Reel Campaign had been subject to surveillance and intelligence-gathering by Undercover Police Officers. They said the surveillance of our Campaign was simply "collateral intrusion". This was the exact term used as if the damage done to us was simply "collateral".

My mind went blank as I did not understand this word. What does it mean? I was still assuming somebody had provided information about Ricky's case until somebody mentioned spying. Why were they spying on me? The thought made me sick. The room started spinning around me and something exploded in my head. I felt other people in the room must have heard the noise. I could not see anyone and was blindsighted.

I am told that John asked the police officers to wait in another room while Suresh fetched me a glass of water. I opened my mouth. No words came out. I pinched my hand then looked at my daughter and tried to touch her to make sure I was alive. She had that concerned look on her face she always has for me. I put my head on the table and started taking deep breaths.

When I was well enough to continue with the meeting, the police officers spoke but the only phrase I heard was "collateral intrusion". I remember wrapping my cardigan very tightly around me. Someone had ripped me open and exposed my innards to the public along with the pain and grief which I try to hide. I don't recall how I returned home.

How would I drop this further bombshell on my family? How was I going to tell them that whilst we were grieving Ricky's loss, trying desperately to find answers to his death, the police had infiltrated our lives as spies? When I told Balwant he asked me why the police did this as we had done nothing wrong. I had no answer, I still have no answer!

I started reading about spying as I was not aware of this practice adopted by the police and wanted to know more about why and how we came under their radar.

The Herne Report cites officer A's claim in an *Observer* article of March 2010 that the SDS officers targeted black campaigns that had been formed in response to deaths in police custody, police shootings or following serious assaults by the police.

Officer "A" states that once the SDS infiltrated an organization, it was effectively finished. This is a serious revelation. Undercover officers are not only "reporting" on campaigns but undermining and sabotaging them from the outset.

The College of Policing Code of Ethics (dated July 2014 page 5, 1.6) says, "covert tactics must be appropriately authorised and any deployments must be shown to be proportionate, lawful, accountable, necessary and ethical".

The pieces of the puzzle started to come together. When we

were begging the police to investigate Ricky's disappearance and death, we were told on several occasions that certain lines of enquiry could not be actioned due to shortage of resources. We now knew resources were being pumped into spying on victims and their families instead of investigating the crimes against them.

We scrabbled around printing appeal posters on our home computer, walking the streets to track down witnesses and CCTV footage, whilst our hearts bled with Ricky's loss. We

Speaking at a meeting of the National Assembly Against Racism. We now know that there were undercover police monitoring these meetings

pleaded with the police to consider Ricky's death as serious while police agents disguised as civilians, were inside our home, at our meetings pretending to support us and others like us. Imposters infiltrated our lives and reported back to their superiors. Is it surprising we have trouble trusting them?

All the flaws found in the police investigation by the Police Complaints Authority—did the police make such significant mistakes like destroying crucial evidence, because they were too busy spying on me?

I thought that the police failings in investigating Ricky's death and the blatant racism we experienced from them was the worst they could do to us. They could not let us down anymore—the damage was surely done? But I was wrong. We were now being asked to take on board that 17 years earlier we had been spied upon!

On 19 June 2014 I was provided with heavily redacted extracts from 13 SDS Intelligence Reports dating between 1998 and 2000. This disclosure was incomplete because on 18th July 2014 I met with officers from Operation Herne and was given conflicting information about the "intelligence" obtained and retained by the Metropolitan Police, who were unaware of the meeting between my family and the Police Herne Team.

We received a formal apology from the Metropolitan Police Assistant Commissioner via a letter dated 12th June 2015, a one-page apology issued so long after the relevant events and as a result of public revelations and outcry about what was already known about the activities of Undercover Police Operations that is entirely inadequate to us.

On 19th June 2015 I met with police officers of the Inquiry Team at New Scotland Yard. John, Suresh and Mon were also present at this meeting. Perhaps of more concern than the incomplete disclosure and flawed process were the reassurances the police officers purported to give: that the intrusion into my family had been collateral and minimal and was, at best, misleading and of no worth to the family at all.

In July 2015 I was told by the Metropolitan Police that there were still 13 Intelligence Reports on the family. Our family has no reason to believe that this is the full extent of the surveillance and records we have been subjected to.

On 18 September 2015, Mr Mike Schwarz, our solicitor, wrote to the Undercover Police Inquiry that some members of my family wished to be Core Participants in the Inquiry. A Core Participant is a person who has played, or may have played a direct and significant role in the subject the Inquiry relates to.

Core Participants are designated by the Chairman, with their consent. In this Inquiry there are two primary categories of Core Participants. State Core Participants: this includes Police Officers, Police Institutions and Government. Non-state Core Participants: this includes individuals that have had relationships with Undercover Officers, trade union members and activists. I am a Core Participant in this Inquiry together with my daughter. Mike Schwarz has now become a dear friend. I don't think I would have known what to do with all the issues that are coming out of this Inquiry but he keeps me in the "loop". When I get frustrated either with the long delay, wondering whether after going through hell and a lot of work, I would be able to take part in this Inquiry and would be given answers to all my questions, Mike in his usual calm manner explains everything. His understanding and advice acts like a balm to my wounded heart. He knows what I am going through and how hard the revelation of spying has hit me and my family.

I feel strongly about this Inquiry and I hope that the Chair can answer our concerns. I wanted to know that as our case was treated in a racially prejudiced manner by the police and their investigation failed us, and this has been accepted and is *referenced in the confidential PCA Report*. I want to know to what extent any undercover policing racially targeted us as we are a Black Justice Campaign and is a relevant question.

I set up a campaign to get justice for my son. I was trying everything possible to seek justice, so there was no justification to spy on me.

I have asked to what extent the undercover policing may have impacted upon and damaged the live investigation into Ricky's death. Ricky's killers still remain at large. During the investigation, many aspects of the investigation work were badly bungled by the police. For example CCTV evidence given to the police by the family was later destroyed by the Met Police without ever being viewed. It held crucial information about the last movements of Ricky. I am concerned that instead of focusing on the Investigation, the police were focusing on spying instead.

I need to know whether the officers dealing with Ricky's case were also the Undercover Police Officers involved with the family or Justice for Ricky Reel Campaign.

Our family, Mike, John and Suresh met with Sir John Mitting (the Chair) on 17 May 2018 at Portcullis House, part of the House of Commons, London. We explained our concerns to him. I said that if the role of Undercover Policing was to prevent and detect crime, why was our Campaign and family the subject of Undercover Policing? Also I should be given all information gathered on me, my family, and Campaign without any redaction to enable me to fully participate in the Inquiry. How can this Inquiry get to the truth without telling me the names of the Undercover Police Officers who spied on me? Sir John told me that I would be fast tracked for disclosure on account of my health. After waiting for 16 months, we received some Reports on 11 September 2019. The Inquiry confirmed that they had not, even with that disclosure, provided everything. To date I have received no further disclosure despite promises made to do so.

I believe we are the first family to be given disclosure by the Inquiry. It is truly baffling to understand why they were spying on me and kept the reports for more than 20 years. Were these going to be used against the family to discredit the Campaign, when the inquest into Ricky's death held on 1 November 1999 at Fulham Town Hall, the press and public who watched it from the Public Gallery observed—that it was as though the Campaign's credibility was on trial. So I ask myself, was this why we were spied upon? To damage our position at the inquest to assist the police to secure "an accidental death" verdict?

I believe that Ricky's murderers have not been caught as resources were transferred to spy on me rather than finding his killers, but then of course they never believed he was murdered The Justice for Ricky Reel Campaign became quite powerful and people are still asking questions about the botched investigation. I am repeatedly asked why the police spied on us almost every day from different people but how can I answer this question when I don't have an answer myself. So what exactly did the SDS officers plan to gain from following my movements? Reading these reports left a sour taste in my mouth. My trust and confidence in people has now been shaken and I ask questions about everybody's intention as to why they want to get involved in this case. This is completely opposite to what I was like before this revelation occurred. Lots of people contact me but the question mark still hangs in the air—who are they really? How many more hurdles do I have to cross to become a whole person again?

Several things are now clear as day to me:

1. We were spied upon at a time when we were vulnerable, shattered by Ricky's death. We were at our lowest ebb, willing to welcome anyone into our lives who offered even the faintest glimmer of hope in our attempt to get answers. The police took advantage of this to infiltrate our lives. The State intruded into our personal lives.

2. The intrusion was neither collateral nor justified. Everything we did was lawful and peaceful. When we picketed, we sought permits. When we set up stalls in Kingston or anywhere else to appeal to the public, we sought permission from the Council. When we sought to make changes to public policy we launched petitions. We were a family fighting for justice. We were not suspects in Ricky's death—our movements had nothing to do with the investigation into his death.

3. The only reason why we were spied upon, in my opinion, is because the police were concerned that the Justice for Ricky Reel Campaign had a huge amount of public support and interest, and they were worried that all of their errors, the racism we had experienced at their hands, would be exposed. Over the years, decades, I have learned that the police appear to be as concerned about their own reputation as anything else. Justice campaigns, by definition, have to challenge and criticise police actions and investigations. This may be one reason why we were targeted.

4. The spying in my view negatively impacted on the investigation into Ricky's death.

Finally, I understood the "click" of the telephone at the end of my calls. I believe the police were probably recording or listening to my telephone calls. I mentioned it to Suresh and my family but then thought perhaps there was something wrong with the telephone line even though it continued for quite some time. The Inquiry has said that intercepted communications/phone tapping is normally outside its remit. (see-https://www.ucpi.org.uk/wp-content/uploads/2020/10/20201014-chairmans-statement-IPA-2016.pdf).

I am concerned that the Chair has, as a general rule, ruled this out. It is important in my case that it is considered as this is part of a pincer movement of spying on me—UCOS being one aspect, potential phone tapping being another. Presumably the information obtained from both sources was shared, e.g. by Special Branch. And to what end?

Similarly, as I was followed by plain clothes officers, presumably from Special Branch, I need to know the whole truth, about what the State did and did not do against me (of which undercover policing is one component part) in order to achieve some sort of peace.

Policing is to detect and prevent crime. Our Campaign, meetings and events were entirely peaceful at all times and we did not associate or work with individuals who had interests in the perpetration of crime. I now ask why was the Justice for Ricky Reel Campaign and my family the subject of undercover policing? This suggests that undercover policing far exceeded any possible legitimate remit.

I am rather concerned that once more the date of our hearing within the Public Inquiry has been delayed. This causes me to wonder as I am getting older whether I will be around to attend this hearing and give evidence and hold the police to account. This was the reason I asked Sir John Mitting to consider appointing a Panel of Advisors who could assist him with his workload and ensure the Inquiry is speedily dealt with in a transparent way, in the way the Stephen Lawrence Inquiry was assisted by a panel. Diverse perspectives and backgrounds make better panels. Sir John is an old white establishment figure and, as with the McPherson Inquiry, the Chair would be assisted in assessing some aspect of the Inquiry's evidence, e.g. racism and criticisms of the police, by having support from others, a panel, with more life experiences, who would really understand what it is like to be ignored or be treated like a second class citizen just because your colour is brown or black. The Inquiry needs to address what it is like to be disregarded simply because I am a woman.

My Barrister in the Inquiry is Mr Matthew Ryder QC. He also represents many other Core Participants affected in different ways by undercover policing, including other family justice campaigns.[4] I quote some sections as follows (Family Justice Campaigns section, from p25):

> *150. There was no reason for there to be any undercover policing of the Reel family campaign, it was not associated with any form of violence or criminality. The fact that UCOs conducted surveillance on the campaign suggests that undercover policing exceeded any possible legitimate remit.*

> *151. Discovering they were subject to undercover policing, on top of Ricky's death and the failed police investigation, has had a serious impact on the family's mental health. The family initially placed trust in police to find those who killed their son. That trust was abused by those who spied on them. That police resources— seemingly unavailable to provide an adequate investigation of his death—were nonetheless available to spy on the family is difficult to comprehend.*

> *152. The family look to this Inquiry to thoroughly examine all aspects of what happened as a first step towards enabling the family to understand how and why they have been let down so badly for so long.*

I feel the Inquiry is geared more towards the rights of violators than to the rights of the violated. I feel Anonymity Orders are dished out to police officers like sweets, but my name and other CPs names will be in the public domain for all to see. The Inquiry is an exercise by the State to protect its own practices while giving the appearance of being a Public Inquiry. While parts of the Inquiry evidence gathering process is being held in public, there are parts from which the public are entirely excluded— so called "closed" hearings, where UCOs with full anonymity (over both real and cover names) are giving evidence. There has been one such hearing already—"tranche 1, phase 4". There are likely to be more and more given so many "recent" UCOs have this sort of protection.

This Inquiry, which started in 2015, was supposed to take three years. It is scheduled to last at least three or four more years. The very least the State can do is to show that they were wrong to spy on ordinary people like us and are taking speedy action to show that the wrong they did years ago is finally put right. Spying has destroyed many lives and the State has a duty to make us whole again. We have waited for 24 years to find how Ricky died and we remain "in limbo". I suffer from health problems since Ricky's death which are compounded by the revelation of Police Spying. This delay only exacerbates this and prolongs the trauma.

We do not, however, want speed for its own sake. We do not want the Inquiry to do its work quickly if that means that it does not get to the truth. That, after all, seems to be precisely what the police would want. I and others are conscious that the announcement of the decision to establish the Inquiry was made in March 2015 by Theresa May, who was, at the time, Home Secretary[5] and the first Chair made his opening remarks at the beginning of the inquiry in July 2015.[6]

The Home Office is the department which "sponsors" the Undercover Policing Inquiry. It funds the Inquiry and the current Home Secretary is ultimately responsible for it. What is often overlooked is that the Home Office seems also to have been the main government department to be responsible for undercover policing—for establishing, funding and supervising the undercover police units. Both the Home Office and the Inquiry itself must be concerned that the Inquiry may last even longer than the Saville Inquiry into Bloody Sunday, currently the longest public inquiry I'm aware of. Set up in April 1998 it lasted for 12 years.[7]

Will costs and corners be cut in order to fit the Home Office's budget, reduce embarrassment all round and ensure that the UCPI concludes before its 12th anniversary, in 2027?

I was just starting to take tiny steps to move forward in my life but the revelation of spying brought me back to 14 October, 1997. Time stood still for me. I felt I was caught up in some time frame where I was searching for Ricky. My mind kept on playing all the things I did in the first seven days when Ricky went missing. It felt like it happened only yesterday. The wounds I was trying to heal opened up and started to bleed again and the grief once more has become unbearable. I started seeing eyes everywhere. Every time I go out I feel that eyes are following me. Many times I have seen police officers near my home and I wonder whether they are watching me or are there for legitimate reasons. I try not to get paranoid as this is not what I was like before the spying. I feel my whole body has been x-rayed through someone's eyes, my stability and my very being has been violated by other people at a time when I was dealing with Ricky's death.

Not knowing that at every stage of my life someone near me was watching and listening to what I was talking about, Thinking about it makes my body go rigid. The nightmares began again. Numerous times my son had calmed me during the night when he hears my screams. When I do manage to fall asleep due to sheer exhaustion, I have dreams that I am running away because someone is chasing me. All I can see is big eyes. I am exhausted all the time because the thought of spying does not let me function during the day time and does not let me sleep at night. As a result, I find it hard to concentrate most of the time. This feeling started to play havoc with my mental and physical health, which started deteriorating very fast. There were times I thought I was dying. I had to pull out of the public eye otherwise I would have died and I wanted to live to get justice for my Ricky.

The identities of police officers are being withheld from the public whilst my life has been stolen by these officers. I did not kill my son. This crime happened outside on the streets of Kingston upon Thames. But these "spies" intruded into my house, life and thoughts. The only reason this Inquiry broke into the public domain, forcing the establishment of the Pitchford Inquiry (now under Sir John Mitting), was because of the relentless campaign by activists and investigative journalists. Ordinary people like me are forced to become activists and campaigners. It is not what I wanted to be, but the system and the institutions forced me to become one in order to ensure that my voice is heard.

Was seeking justice for my son a crime? And by doing so, was I causing any harm to anyone? Was I putting this country's security at risk? Am I being punished for raising my voice against the mistakes made by the police?

I feel my life does not belong to me anymore because SDS officers were ordered to intrude into my life! Who ordered it and why? We all need answers so that this practice does not happen again. I feel on edge all the time, irritable, unable to concentrate, as I feel someone is hovering around me, but out of sight. I wonder what risks writing this book will entail.

My wounds are deep and they continue to bleed, and the absence of truth and justice nearly destroyed me. There is no peace without justice and I long for peace. But now knowing that SDS officers were spying on me and my family is almost killing me. The State did this and almost destroyed me and now the State has a duty to make me whole again.

Chapter 7

Reflections on the investigation—Our experiences of police institutional racism

Racism and justice collided one day
Unfortunately, racism came to the top
My fight for my son Ricky
Will continue and I will not let it drop

Racism played a big part in this case. Ricky's case started with racist abuse which quickly culminated in a racist attack and his death. In my view the case was initiated by police officers who displayed racist views or opinions from day one. No matter what I did, I was unable to change their views, formed by the police officers within minutes of recovering Ricky's body on 21 October 1997 from the river in Kingston upon Thames, without carrying out any forensic tests or enquiries. The police assumed that Ricky had fallen into the river while urinating and closed this case as an "accident".

In the early days I did a lot of research on the computer, read books or simply talked to people to get advice. I came across this research paper by Dean Jones called *Fatal Call: Getting Away With Murder,* which states:

> *The opposite of case construction is 'case denial' where the investigator forms an early view that no crime has been committed, which can limit the investigation to proving that 'no offence took place'. Indeed, this is what happened in the case of Ricky Reel who went missing in 1997 but whose family still campaigns for justice.*
>
> *When this youth was reported missing, the police took the view that there was no crime even after his body was found in the River Thames, Such preconceived views on the part of investigators can lead to "premature closure" of investigations prior to all reasonable lines of inquiry being followed in accordance with Section 23a of the Criminal Procedures and Investigations Act 1996. Again, both case denial and premature closure are relevant to decision making at the scenes of death..*
>
> *I feel that a failure to identify a homicide, thereby allowing someone to "get away with murder", is a miscarriage of justice in its own right.[8]*

In Ricky's case it appears the police clung to the "tunnel vision". I say this because from the first day the police officers formed their own opinion about what happened to Ricky and they believed they were right even when evidence pointed to the contrary or had not been adequately gathered, or gathered then lost.

Convinced of a belief without exploring alternative views is a major cause of miscarriages of justice. The racial attack prior to his disappearance points to the likelihood that Ricky had been killed. All our efforts were unable to shift the views of the investigating officers.

It is stated in *Policing and the Legacy of Lawrence* that:

> *... between 1998 and the end of 1999, policing in London faced an onslaught of high profile critical incidents. It was a very testing period for the police in London. Amongst the usual policing demands were incidents that ran and ran in the national press throughout the year. One of them was also the Ricky Reel Investigation. Scotland Yard's reputation for professional investigation was in tatters, Stephen's case having been linked in the public consciousness with Michael Menson and Ricky Reel 'failed' investigations. The conclusion drawn from all the evidence in connection with the racist murder are clear. There was no doubt that there were fundamental errors as the investigation was marred by a combination of professional incompetence, institutional racism and a failure of leadership by senior officers. This was also repeated in Ricky's case and later confirmed in the secret PCA Report. Due to this and the time factor the second investigation could not salvage the mistakes made in the first investigation.*[9]

Thus the Ricky Reel case remains 'open' and is left to my family and supporters to find more evidence which could give us answers.[10]

I am not surprised after reading a report where the writer stated:

> *In the mid 1990s Kingston upon Thames experienced one of the worst periods when within two years two people from black and minority ethnic (BME) backgrounds were presumed murdered because of their race. He said he was particularly astonished by the lack of urgency in the response from the MPS (Metropolitian Police Service) to the murder of these young black people and appalled by the resistance to investigate these racist crimes. He further stated that during the Stephen Lawrence Inquiry*

> *he became frustrated and disappointed at the evidence*
> *of so many police officers and was appalled by the*
> *contempt shown by them.*

This was going on at the same time of Ricky's death. No wonder we were also treated like we were nothing, our lives do not matter because of the colour of our skin.

The Macpherson Report was highly critical of the

Speaking at a conference about the #spycops scandal

Metropolitian police officers who investigated the Lawrence murder. It said:

> *The investigation was marred by a combination of*
> *professional incompetence, institutional racism and*
> *a failure of leadership by senior officers", and right at*
> *the same time this was also happening in the Ricky Reel*
> *case.*[11]

Recently the media has highlighted all the mistakes made and the attitudes of the police in different cases and I wonder when it will change. I am not saying all police officers are "bad" but the saying that one bad apple contaminates the whole barrel seems to apply here. It doesn't give me much hope as similar mistakes are still repeated.

The challenge for the government and the police is to maintain and improve public trust and confidence in the police.

The public has a right to expect that those who uphold the law on their behalf are held to account when their actions are called into question.

I see no point in having public inquiries when the outcome or the recommendations are not taken on by the police.

McPherson's definition of racial incident, "a racial incident is any incident which is perceived to be racist by the victim or any other person", was totally ignored by the police even though a police officer knew about the racist attack before me. In fact he was the first person to tell me about it, so surely he understood that Ricky and his friends were subjected to this racial attack and Ricky, who was missing, was in danger. Policies are there for guidance but ignored once the inquiries end. Even the Scarman Report, released on 25 November, 1981, stressed the importance of tackling racial disadvantage and racial discrimination.[12]

For my family the pain of injustice has compounded this tragedy. Not simply because the loss itself is unbearable but also because the quest for justice had been made very difficult due to initial police inaction to achieve this.

I try not to become bitter and sometimes I think that at least I was lucky to have Ricky for 20 years.

But the pain that goes away for a few seconds returns and rips my body apart. The anger still rages inside me. Ricky's departure from my world, my arms, crystallised in my mind that injustice exists, that the colour of his skin and ours prevented even to this day in getting justice for my son and his family. I am of the opinion that the colour of skin affects life chances.

Racism is irrational, ignorant and cowardly but it is deadly. Unless we challenge it, it will continue to get worse. I know the pain I and my family had suffered and for that reason I decided to challenge it. It was not easy to do that but I thought by challenging it, other families would be spared the indifference, stereotyping and question marks over their race and culture.

It has now almost been 25 years since Ricky died. The Justice for Ricky Reel Campaign has gone on for longer than

Ricky was actually alive. All I and my family ever wanted was to find out how Ricky died. His death was long after Stephen Lawrence's death and the treatment I received was long after the MacPherson Report.

The question that needs to be asked is whether a white middle class family would have been treated the same way as my family has been treated.

The Macpherson Report made many recommendations. It also stated that an incident is racist if it is perceived to be racist by the victim or any other person. It is ironic that it took a Judge to educate the police about how to identify racism after a tragic death.

Whenever I see or hear news about any racial attack which the police had not investigated properly, a sigh escapes my lips and I murmur how many more? After each and every case it is said that police have learned lessons. But the question is when will they learn lessons? And I ask what had happened to all the lessons they said they have learned from previous cases, but still continue to make the same mistakes. How many more lessons need to be learned?

Quite a lot of cases coming after Ricky have suffered the same fate. What does each and every death teach the police? If lessons were learned after Stephan Lawrence's death, why were the same mistakes repeated in Ricky's death. Was it ignorance, laziness or just black lives do not matter?

There are cases of racism all over the country which we all hear about. I would like to believe that racism is decreasing but reading and hearing about so many cases where people were subjected to violence or threats of violence simply due to their colour or religion I think it is on the rise.

In the wake of Covid 19, we know racial crimes increased exponentially, and some of the main victims? BAME doctors, nurses, health professionals on the front line. It is on the rise, and we have the opportunity now to do something about it.

We were racially stereotyped and just not given the level of investigation Ricky's death should have received because we are Asian, and I believe it was assumed by the police that we would not question them. Our race and culture became a barrier which they failed to understand.

Hate crimes can happen anywhere. It is just people's perception that hate crimes happen in industrial areas or poor council areas. This is just a myth. Ricky died in Kingston upon Thames, a hugely affluent area. Racism transcends all classes, all socio-economics backgrounds. It is important that every community should support all cases like this and other victims irrespective of their colour.

The Asian community as a body was not as vocal 25 years ago when Ricky died. Now the community is stronger, but we need to prove to the authorities who still don't take us seriously, that we will stand together—we have new social media platforms that we can use to make our views known. Let's use them.

The police need to regain public confidence. This will not happen till there is accountability and transparency—and we do not have these yet.

Inquests need to be carried out sympathetically. They need to remember that the family sitting there listening to what happened to their loved ones, should be treated with respect rather than be asked questions which are not relevant to the case. I feel my visit to the Lawrence Inquiry should not have been questioned, as I went there to support the Lawrence family as I do with other families.

Inquests are held to determine the cause of the death and not to insult or belittle families as I had watched my Ricky's life belittled, cheapened and played down as to why he went missing in the first place. Memories of Ricky are all I have now and even those I believe are not safe.

Legal Aid should have been provided to us, because not only I had to find funds to cover the legal costs but had to bare the humiliation of asking supporters to raise funds.

Having been supported by so many people, I realise how vital it is to people to know that someone cares and is willing to help. For me race and culture do not matter as I see people simply as human beings.

Ricky's death has made changes in the Missing Persons Policy. I was told that each and every case will be looked at on its own merit. Some positive changes. I was told that with the new policy Ricky's case would have been looked at with high priority.

The new policy states:

> *The call handler is the first point of contact in missing persons cases. The level and the quality of information obtained is crucial in determining the appropriate response. Call handlers are the first to assess the level of risk and identify the urgency of the response required. All call handlers should, therefore, receive appropriate training in identifying and understanding risk and risk factors... Hate crimes may be, or may become critical incidents regardless of how trivial an incident may initially appear.*

It took a death to show the authorities what are hate crimes and how these cases should be investigated when it was quite straightforward that we were saying exactly that as Ricky and friends were called racist names and later attacked.

Families in our situation are too often left to pick up the pieces of their loss and a failed police investigation in isolation. In these situations, with no support, these families are worn down gradually by the hostility of the police.

But the experience of my family is living proof that having the support and backing of others can make a world of difference to bereaved families. It's the difference between having to accept the authorities' answers as final because people have no strength left to fight or an easy way out because you do not have the will to fight or live. Having the support means you can challenge the excuses that families are too often given.

If anything positive can be gleaned from my experience, it

is that as long as there are people who have the courage and commitment to support families like ours, then the authorities will never be able to remain complacent about the murder of a loved one or leave that family at the mercy of the authorities in solitude. The police need to take action where necessary straight away, irrespective of the victim's colour or religion.

The impact of hate crime talks should start with schools. We all have seen that quite a few children have been subjected to violence or name calling and as a result have taken their own lives because they felt nobody was listening to them. For them the only option to stop this bullying was to end their lives. This education is necessary to stop race attacks or killings and hopefully stop this at a very early stage.

Losing a child is something you never overcome—and it is near impossible to overcome without knowing who killed Ricky, without the police offering to reinvestigate from the beginning and with an open mind using new technology. All we can do is keep pressing for answers in the hope that if something like this were to happen again, the police won't treat that family or victim with the racism and disregard that they treated us.

As a family we work together to try and create change.

My family lives with this traumatic loss every day and we are unable to grieve for Ricky until justice is delivered. The numerous public meetings, the leafleting, standing outside Scotland Yard screaming for justice, processions in Kingston, fastings and the vigils highlighted Ricky's case all over the world.

Soon after Ricky's death I decided I wanted to visit India, especially the Golden Temple. I was hurt and trying to find solace. People in the plane and in India recognised me and knew about Ricky's case and I later found out that the media in India had covered the case. I get calls and messages of support from all over the world, and this was due to everybody's efforts to try to get justice for my son.

There is a memorial plaque for Ricky on the wall of the Golden Temple in Amritsar, India, where thousands of people visit to pay their homage. There is no peace in our minds or hearts as Ricky's killers are still out and the fear is that they may strike again and somebody else may become their victim.

All this happened because priority was given to spying on us rather than investigating Ricky's case and this has exacerbated our pain, grief and loss.

Plaque erected in memory of Ricky in the Golden Temple at Amritsar

We are told that the investigation into Ricky's death remains open and the police will follow any new lines of enquiry coming into their attention. However it is quite clear that the police are not looking into any new lines of enquiry and will only react to any information which I, my family or the public can provide! That had been the case all along. It is important to keep Ricky's memory alive and to continue to highlight the inequalities and the injustices in the criminal justice system.

Chapter 8

The present and the roadmap for the future

I have travelled many miles, over many years
Searching for the answers that would give me peace
Mile after mile as my feet hit the ground
Hour after hour with a longing that won't cease.

Ricky died almost 25 years ago and the road ahead is still very dark.

At every corner I miss seeing and hugging Ricky but, strangely, I feel his presence all the time. It is as if he is asking me to get the justice I promised him years ago.

My family suffered a double tragedy—the loss of a son and a brother and the failure of the authorities to catch his killers.

Injustice heaped upon injustice. His death has not gone unheeded or unheard. It has, through the Justice for Ricky Reel Campaign, become a call for action. Action against racism. Ricky's death will leave a legacy; a society free of racism and racist policing.

14 October is known as Ricky Reel Day. Many people will

pray for you to rest in peace.

My children have grown up but we still all talk about Ricky as if he is still with us. Hundreds of people contact us. They want to help to find out how he died. The majority of people have said that Ricky's death was a racist murder and the police investigation was not done properly. Lack of a proper investigation is the main reason why Ricky has been denied justice.

Supporters leave messages on my Facebook, send emails, tweets or telephone me directly. It gives me courage to continue with my fight for justice for Ricky.

This case has been raised in Parliament many times. I recently did some live programmes and interviews on zoom due to Covid and all the listeners offered support. They were quite surprised to note that I am still struggling to find justice for Ricky after 24 years. They feel that with modern technology the police should once more try to find how Ricky died.

My supporters requested that I create a petition which everybody will sign to demand a new investigation into Ricky's case. Again, after discussing with Suresh, John and Mon and my family, I decided to create the petition my supporters want. Supporters can share and sign it at *http://chng.it/MnqqMkLvwH*. I also believe with new technology the photographs and other evidence can be enhanced to review the case.

Allegiances or relationships change and every day I hope someone will speak and tell me who killed my son and why. This has now become my life's mission. I believe that the truth always surfaces in the long run and I am confident that Ricky's case is no exception to that.

Ricky's name is now remembered by thousands of people all over the world. Ricky's death has not served in the interests of racists. His name is mentioned in many books, reports, policies and procedures. It has united black and white people in anger and determination. It has not cowed or weakened black or Asian people, but made them stronger.

Ricky's death not only united people of all colours, castes, faiths and religions but offered courage to all those who grieve in silence. It has given people courage to speak out and demand justice to any wrong doings they have suffered.

Ricky in death has shown people that we cannot be complacent in the face of indifference. Sometimes it is ok to stand up and ask questions to find the truth.

Racism itself is a lie and those who know the truth will always fight and defeat that lie. The pain inflicted by racism can be life long and unbearable. Racism is an underlying evil that stains our society, where a person's skin colour becomes an excuse for them to be insulted, harassed, attacked or killed.

For everyone the name of Ricky Reel stands for justice unfulfilled, the hurt of loss amplified by the lasting anguish of a crime unresolved. From our continuing search for truth and justice our family and supporters will not let official complacency obliterate injustice.

Ricky's name has become one of the symbols that demands justice. The catalyst begun by the Campaign for Justice for Ricky Reel produced a lasting momentum for justice. Without this the Civil Rights Caravan would not have had a scheduled stop in Plymouth. Nor would anti-racists have travelled from Plymouth to Prague to charge Europe's institutions and employers with racism. Plymouths' initiatives put Ricky's case forward internationally, starting with Holland.

I keep asking questions. I live in a democratic society upon which the rest of the world looks with veneration. I live in a judicial system which the world looks upon to adopt. I live in a society where the police at one time were held with the highest regard. So what is the problem? Why did the police and the judicial system fail me?

Was Ricky's life expendable because of his colour or was he the victim of fun for a few who have no regard for life? No, Ricky's life was not expendable nor was he prey for the hunt.

The question then arises, how do we end racism from our society? We all have a duty to educate our children, family and friends that whenever racism rears its ugly head it leaves nothing but devastation in its wake. We may be of different colour, religion or faith but underneath the skin we are all the same. Everybody's blood is red.

It is important that if the public and in particular the ethnic minority communities are to have confidence in the police, then the police need to change their attitudes and policies and ensure they deliver equal justice. They need to learn about different cultures and understand them. They need to believe people when crimes are reported and investigate them with an open mind.

I have to accept that the aching pain I feel in my heart every day is here to stay forever. I have had to come to terms with the fact that my life will always be missing a huge piece and therefore it will always be incomplete. Somehow I have managed to create an invisible wall between myself and other people and feel that I cannot participate in the things I used to do before Ricky's death. I find no joy in the things which used to make me laugh out loud before.

Sometimes I wish I could return to my life before Ricky's death but unfortunately my son's death and everything that I had to endure has made it difficult to resume that part of my life. I have to live with the emotional scars for the rest of my life and I have realised that this is something I cannot change but must learn to accept since none of this is in my hands

I cannot bring Ricky back, no matter how hard I try. But getting justice for Ricky and other victims is within my control. Injustices and prejudices are not something we have to learn to live with and accept; it is something that collectively we have the strength and courage to fight against. The tenacity shown by all those who have joined my family in my fight for justice is proof of this.

One of the hardest things about losing a child is the feeling of helplessness, that I was unable to protect Ricky during those last moments of his life. Most parents live with this guilt no matter how their child dies. I also live with this guilt every day.

I spent years planning Ricky's future with him, yet all it took was a few moments and he was snatched from my arms forever. Every night thousands of parents all over the world wait for their children to return home and every night a few of those parents will be left waiting for the rest of their lives in vain unless we all fight for our rights and justices.

Every time I see Ricky's empty bed, his clothes, I am reminded of what I have lost. But I am also reminded of what other parents stand to lose if the present complacent attitude of society in general and the authorities specifically is allowed to go unchallenged.

It sickens me every time I hear about other families who have suffered what we have and I think to myself, how this can still be happening? I was told the mistakes in previous cases would not be repeated in mine but unfortunately they were. Then I hear of another family who have lost a loved one in similar circumstances, almost identical to Ricky's death, and are being met with the same hostility from the police that we faced, and continue to face. I am just horrified by the fact that the same cycle is repeating itself over and over again.

None of us can afford to turn our heads or hearts from the problem of racism because it is unavoidable. It is this knowledge which drives my struggle for justice for my son. It is my tribute to Ricky that the cause for which he died has been and continues to be fought for bravely and persistently, irrespective of the trauma I am going through.

There are many emotional wounds that will never be healed, loss of family time, siblings getting married without Ricky and living with an ache that he will never see their children. The road ahead is bleak, but even with a weakened body I tread on, hoping I can get justice for Ricky and finally give him peace and the rest of my family can move on. I can look at myself in the mirror and say "I have finally fulfilled my promise to you my Ricky".

Ricky's death and our fight for justice has brought many changes.

I was told that the Missing Persons Policy has changed as a result of this case. In Ricky's case the first police officer on the scene believed that as an adult Ricky should not immediately be regarded as a missing person. Accordingly, he did not immediately record the racial incident or complete a missing persons report.

The Metropolitan Policy categorised missing persons as "vulnerable" or "non vulnerable" purely on the basis of age, so Ricky was classified as "non vulnerable" as he was over the age of 18. Had a fuller account of Ricky's disappearance been taken at the time, he would have been considered "vulnerable" regardless of his age. It is recommended that in future the classification of "vulnerable" and "non vulnerable" be based on all the attendant circumstances.

Whenever I see a police appeal for a missing person or an incident room set up to investigate a crime or a reconstruction, I always have the same thought: Why wasn't this done for my son? At the same time, I feel comforted that Ricky's death has changed this practice. This means in future a coordinated investigation rather than an ad hoc one will be done, which will ensure that all investigations are carried out properly and all police members of the team are aware of each other's responsibility.

West Drayton and Kingston police placed different interpretations on police force policy in respect of who was responsible for the missing persons enquiry. West Drayton considered that Kingston police should investigate both the missing person report and the racial incident, on the grounds that the two events were linked and both happened in Kingston. However, Kingston decided that they were responsible for investigating the racial incident but that West Drayton police were responsible for the missing persons inquiry since Ricky lived in that area.

In Detective Superintendent Mr Morgan's view, the two events were linked, but only insofar as the racial incident caused Ricky to become separated from his friends. He decided that West Drayton was responsible for the missing persons enquiry while Kingston were responsible for the racial incident.

It is recommended that in future due regard should

be given to the best location for detection when allocating missing person enquiries to a particular force area and that the emphasis should be on the collation of information and coordinated action.

The Surrey report found that there was poor communication between different groups of police officers involved in the case and between police officers and members of my family, with the result that numerous officers contacted me between 17 and 19 October 1997 and gave me conflicting information about what action was being taken.

Accordingly, the force should now review their communication strategy and policies for all prolonged or complex investigations, whether they are classified as major or not. The strategy should require proper lines of communication to be established with the victim's family.

At the time there was no process with the Metropolitan Police Service for selection or training of Family Liaison Officers. To compound this, our Family Liaison Officer was not properly briefed before she came to inform my children of Ricky's death, in my absence.

It is recommended that a proper selection process be implemented to identify appropriate officers and also adequate training and support are provided. As their roles are crucial in cases like mine, the officers involved must be aware of their roles and responsibilities.

I also recommended changing their role at the McPherson Inquiry. The role at the time caused nothing but heartache and anguish. I also stated they should be briefed about the case before contacting the victims and not just be planted in their home to gather "intelligence" or act like "spies".

It has been suggested that the role of "consultant" should be abandoned and that Area Major Incident Pool's terms of reference should be clearly set out in any such future enquiries.

We were told that PC Peters, when talking to Dean, did not believe that he was reporting a racial incident when describing the confrontation with the white youths because Dean only referred to it in passing. I fail to understand this as PC Peters told me that Ricky and his friends were racially attacked but failed to log this incident. A racial attack is an attack no matter how small or big.

The counter clerk misguidedly believed that the Asian culture forbade the drinking of alcohol or associating with people outside that culture. This clearly influenced his approach to the report of Ricky's disappearance.

I was told that the PCA will be emphasising the need for supervising officers in the Metropolitan Police to ensure that all racial incidents are fully recorded regardless of how they are brought to police attention. They would also be recommending that in future, culture awareness training should acknowledge that different members of the same culture may observe different behavioural norms.

The above changes to the Metropolitan Police Policy and Procedures are the result of the Justice for Ricky Reel Campaign because I matter, my son matters and we deserve equal rights. I hope that with these changes, any future cases like mine are treated with respect and dignity.

I hope that parents' voices are heard and believed rather than ignored like mine, and assumptions that I did not know my own son would not be repeated as I felt I was being insulted. I hope proper and meaningful support is provided by the police to victims and their families.

Ricky took part in sports. This was confirmed by his school reports and other correspondence. Yet I was asked questions whether I was aware of this! The doctor's report sent to the police confirmed he was fit and healthy. School reports confirmed his activities. Why all the questions when I was the one who cleaned his sports clothes and boots, paid for them and took or dropped him at different venues?!

Since Ricky's death I have been approached by many people doing their own dissection of Ricky's case. The next generation coming behind Ricky are going to remember him and hopefully help in the learning of lessons about what went wrong in Ricky's case and it will not be repeated. My aim is for people of different colour and faith to learn to respect each other. I do not stand by in the face of injustice.

Positive changes can only come through people standing up to powerful institutions. I remain proud of all I have done to raise my son's case and will continue until I get justice for Ricky. I need to understand what happened to him so that lessons are learned by all.

I am labelled a campaigner, activist, or sometimes a troublemaker as I refuse to disappear but it does not bother me. I have always fought for justice and been motivated by a sense of justice all throughout my life. It is at the core of who I am, the one who does not stand idly by in the face of injustice, cruelty, helplessness or any other problem. My profession as a Homeless Persons Officer has taught me many things about dealing with people's problems Compassion and positive help also go hand in hand.

My parents' teachings, "you should neither commit injustice against another nor suffer injustice yourself", played a big part in my life and this fight for justice.

There are plaques in Kingston upon Thames and Hounslow provided by the respective Councils. There is also a plaque on the wall of the Golden Temple in Amritsar in India. My son's plaques are there for people from all colours and faiths. These also remind people of the justice denied to Ricky Reel.

> *This day 25 years ago*
> *You left me and disappeared*
> *Not a day has passed that I've not cried for you*
> *Each year, this day I fear*
>
> *It reminds me that time moves on without you*
> *Creating oceans of time I cannot cross*
> *That you stay the same as I get older*
> *Grieving my treasured child's loss*

It still feels like only yesterday
That I waited and waited at night
For you to walk through the door and see me
And say, "Mum, I'm home, goodnight"

But you never came and I waited still
Seven long days with no word from you
I searched for you everywhere my son
I didn't know what else to do

In bins, in buildings, in dark corners and more
I thought I'd find you hurt but still taking breath
But since that day 25 long years ago
My life has been consumed by your death

The one place I couldn't search my son
Was below the deep water, dark and suffocating
I passed that spot so many times
Little knowing you lay there, patiently, waiting

They told me you were gone that day
Told your brother and sisters too:
"Your brother's body's been found at the bottom of the river"
How could these cruel words be true?

They didn't care how long you'd lain there
They didn't care that you had tried
To come back home and return to me
To simply breathe and stay alive

They wrote you off as one more black youth
Didn't care what had really happened to you
Those racist people had seen only your colour
They didn't see my Ricky, they didn't see you

And the people who were supposed to help us
Find answers and find the truth
They didn't care and wanted me to stay silent
They didn't seek facts, answers or proof

They wanted me to go away and be quiet
Forget what happened to my son
They wanted me to ask no questions
They wanted me to make no noise

No, not me, I'm here to question till the end
I'm here to ask why, when, by whose hand?
I won't go away, not me
My son's life is worth more than you'll understand

My heart has grown cold as that water
That covered you for seven long days
But I will not rest till justice is done
Not me, I am not going away

Chapter 9

Tributes sent by supporters

The Ballad of Ricky Reel
By Mac Rogers

This is the story of Ricky
Who died in Kingston town
Whose body was found in the River Thames,
But no-one saw him drown
SWEET THAMES RUN SOFTLY TILL I END MY SONG!

That fateful night he walked with friends
When some white youths challenged him
But Ricky refused to answer
And the white boys grew grim
The more they shouted, the quicker he ran
The sweat of fear on his brow
He ran to the river in the darkness of night

Could no one help him now?
Where is my wandering son tonight
Where, oh where can he be?
I cannot rest till he comes home Oh bring back my Ricky
to me!
BRING BACK! OH BRING BACK, OH BRING BACK MY
RICKY TO ME
Mrs Reel went to the Met Police
To find her lovely boy
But the Met Police did nothing
To give that mother joy

For the Met Police were racist
The Met Police were slow
The Met Police did nothing at all
They didn't want to know
And Old Father Thames keeps rolling along Down to the
mighty sea

He doesn't seem to worry
Doesn't care for Fortune's Fame
He never seems to hurry
But he gets there just the same
What does he know? What does he care?
Nothing for you or me!
He's just like the Met Police, my friend As anyone can see

What do we want? Justice!
When do we want it? Now!

But they reckoned without Mrs Reel, man
She searched with all her might
They twiddled their thumbs in the night time
They sit on their arses by day
They mistakenly thought
if they buried their heads

The problem would go away
She walked those ways for days and days
Where Ricky ran that night

BRING BACK! OH BRING BACK, OH BRING BACK MY
RICKY TO ME
Then at last they divers found him
Upon the river bed
His body was there, but his spirit was not
For poor dear Ricky was dead

SWEET THAMES RUN SOFTLY TILL I END MY SONG!
We think that your son was foolish
We think that your son was drunk
He went close to the edge to relieve himself
And in seconds your son had sunk

I swear by the moon that is rising tonight
I swear by the dying sun
I will have justice for you my boy
And I will see it done

SWEET THAMES RUN SOFTLY TILL I END MY SONG!
In seven days they brought him back
They brought him to the door
But it wasn't with joy that she greeted her boy
As they laid him on the floor

"One day your son will be famous
A name that everyone knows"
These were the words Ricky uttered once
But he died 'neath a flurry of blows

Your name it is true My Ricky
Will live on forever and ay
Whenever a black boy is murdered Your image will not

go away

Thank God for the team that supports her
Imran, Louise and John
Suresh and Michael are towers of strength
And his memory lingers on

In the name of Ricky Reel
Let us fight for the right of Justice
And proclaim it with all our might
As we join in the hymn for equality
Enjoyed by both black and white

"All things white and wonderful
All Creatures great and small
All things black and beautiful
The Lord God made them all"
SWEET THAMES RUN SOFTLY AS I END MY SONG!

To Ricky Reel
By Benjamin Zephaniah

I don't know how to say this Ricky
But things are not getting better.
We are trying to protect each other
We are shouting loud on demonstrations
On the streets, in the halls,
And in churches, mosques and temples.
We have done non-violent things
In silence
On the streets, in the halls
And in churches, mosques and temples
I think of you every time I see water gi,
I never saw you fight
But you are a martyr gi,
That river that runs beside my first kiss place
Even that river
Reminds me of you gi.
Now every time I see your mother
I think of womanhood
And every time your mother speaks
I hear her cry,
Things are not getting better Ricky.
The bad news is
Your mother is so special
She is unique and precious
She shines in a galaxy of women
She is a tender one and only,
But there are so many mothers like her,
That's the bad news Ricky,
There are more mothers crying
Things went from bad to worse
And then from worse to this serious sickness.
I have to be really honest with you Ricky man
I don't know who to trust,

I look at white girls and think
Do they want to dance with me or kill me?
I look at white boys and I wonder
Do they want to play football with me
Or drown me?
I look at policemen and wonder what would happen
if I asked them the time?
There is a crisis here,
I'm in trouble Ricky,
I think of you every time I'm out in the dark,
When I see pictures of Marx, Lenin
Or Gandhi
I wonder what can we do for you,
Every time I look at Malcolm X
Clinging to my bedroom wall
I wonder what means are necessary.

There is a great wickedness here
And it thrives on people who do nothing,
It is planted deep in the souls of the serious sick
I don't know how to say this,
But things are certainly not getting better,
The pacifists are out,
The militants are out
And we will not be defeated,
But it's hard, very hard.
I keep seeing your face in my self
And every time I see your mother
There is a constant
I love you Ricky
In her eyes.

Mon Matharu
Uncle of Ricky Reel

Early morning on 15 October, 1997, I received a call from Sukhdev Reel, my sister. She sounded very distressed. She enquired if by any chance Ricky had come over and stayed the night at our house. That straightaway rang warning bells. It was not in Ricky's nature not to tell his parents if he was staying the night out. Indeed, he did not have the habit of staying nights out. Even if he had come over to stay with us, I am certain he would have let his parents know as I myself would have questioned him on this first.

I went straight over to see my sister and gathered whatever information was available. The whole family was very distressed and it hurt to see them in that state. I came home and contacted two of my friends, one a Metropolitan police officer and the other a Scotland Yard detective for their advice. Paying heed to their advice I then collected Balwant Reel, Ricky's dad and visited the Kingston police station for assistance. What transpired from then on is narrated by Sukhdev Reel in her own words. All I will add is that instead of getting assistance at the time of reporting at the Kingston police station, we received all excuses and abuse. I believe to this day that had the Metropolitan Police taken our concerns seriously on that day and acted quickly we may have been able to know what happened to Ricky that night. Two years later at the time of the inquest into the death, the Metropolitan Police went further and instructed the Coroner to refer me to the Director of Public Prosecutions for interfering with police work.

After nearly 25 years we still do not know how Ricky ended up at the bottom of River Thames in Kingston. I continue to live with the hope that we will get to know the truth in my lifetime, which unfortunately is nearing the end.

Ricky, along with all other of my nephews and nieces, was very close to me. More so in that we lived nearby and had family meet ups all the time. Not a single day goes by when Ricky is not in my thoughts and the hurt of losing him burns as harsh as day one. All I have left is his pictures and my happy memories of him growing up.

Mike Schwarz
Solicitor

It is easy to see Sukhdev Reel and her family and supporters as victims. Because they are. They have suffered at the hands of those responsible for Ricky's likely murder, for the botched police investigations, for covert and deplorable policing and cover-ups, some no doubt ongoing. And, yes, Sukhdev and others around her have been damaged by the experience. Who would not be?

But, as this book shows, what stands out is Sukhdev's unshakable resilience and seemingly endless energy and initiative. The result: a decades-long focus on seeking justice— for Ricky and for those responsible for the setbacks and stitch-ups she has endured over the years.

Although Sukhdev's search for the truth is far from done, some facts are established already. She has proved to be a fiercely protective mother and indomitable campaigner. Morally, she is on a different plane to her opponents. Those of us who have had the privilege of seeking to assist her are in awe.

Ricky would, rightly, have been proud of her.

Harbans Bhambra

I am Sukhdev Reel's younger sister and Ricky's aunt. I was living with Sukhdev at the time of Ricky's birth. I have fond memories of Ricky. He was a very happy, calm baby. He was not skinny and his eyes were large and sparkling, but they had this innocent and yet deep look about them. I remember we were all so happy when he was born and I can also say that I had the privilege of baby sitting and holding him on a lot of occasions. When I got married and moved to Hounslow, my children who are younger than Ricky became very close and we used to hang around each other's houses on weekends.

Ricky was a very quiet well-mannered loving child and I do not recall that I ever needed to tell him off for anything. Sukhdev's children and my children grew up together and we all used to spend happy times at my mum's house on some weekends as well.

We moved to Australia in 1993 and my children lost touch with their cousins.

When we returned to London in 1996, my children were very happy to get together with their cousins. I have pictures of Ricky sitting with his siblings and my children at my mum's house and this picture clearly shows the grown-up Ricky, but the smile and those innocent eyes and the round face still are the same as when he was a baby.

That was the last time I saw Ricky in 1996, not aware that I would never see him again. We all have fond memories of Ricky and he will always be in our hearts.

When I received a phone call in October 1997 to say that Ricky was missing, I was shocked and could not think straight. Later I was told that he was dead. At that time, I was unable to travel to attend his funeral because of my own family commitments. However, I was kept informed about everything and Ricky and his family were in my thoughts and prayers at all times. I kept in touch with my sister and my other siblings to keep up to date with any other findings.

When I visited Sukhdev in 2002, I was shocked to see how Ricky's death had left a big void in everyone's lives. When I entered their house and saw Ricky's pictures on the wall, I was so torn up and lost for words. I had no words to comfort my sister and her family because there were no adequate words to comfort them or bring Ricky back. I looked at Ricky's siblings and my heart went out to them.

Even now when I see my sister and her family, I can see the impact of Ricky's death, the effect of the campaign and the scars that have been left on the whole family by the mishandling by the police where they have been totally negligent and insensitive to this matter. To them it may have been nothing, but to my sister's family and all of us it has been an insult and misconduct. I pray no one goes through what Ricky's family have gone through.

A few last words for Ricky:

Dear Ricky, you were like a son to me as we are a close knit family where there is no discrimination between my children or my sibling's children. My heart breaks when I see your mum and dad and I have no words of comfort to offer them. I am proud of your siblings, who have taken a positive approach but they miss you every day. Your mother is just existing and not living as part of her died when you died. She is not the same happy person she used to be. I hope and pray we all get closure soon and the perpetrators are brought to own up to the terrible evil they have done. Your name is known by people all over the world now because your family has been determined to make the world aware of the way your life was taken and the matter was hushed.

Ricky, I promise you one thing as I am sure you are watching over us and I believe Karma will do justice, the people responsible will one day pay for this as their conscience and Karma will not let them sleep at night.

Always in our hearts and may God keep you safe out of this wicked world.

Michael Mansfield QC

A very powerful and moving book. Above all it demonstrates what can be done and achieved by the individual who is collectively supported in a common purpose. A fitting epitaph is that this momentum caught up with Cressida Dick, who was forced to step down after a dismal attempt to distance herself from the Lawrence Inquiry's main finding of "institutional racism" when the full extent of everyday racial prejudice was dramatically exposed at a police station in central London (Charing Cross) and this, with other shortcomings, formed the basis of the Mayor's critique of no confidence. The continuing and increasingly effective struggle, albeit incremental, is testament to you and hundreds of others like you.

Sabby Dhalu
Co-Convenor of Stand up to Racism

Sukhdev Reel's tireless quest for justice for her son Ricky Reel has been an inspiration to many. No one should have to endure what Sukhdev has but the institutional racism that is still alive and kicking today means many still do. Losing a son or daughter is every parent's worst nightmare. Losing one in a racist attack and to then suffer the institutional racism of the police force and the criminal justice system is worse still.

That no one has been brought to justice since Ricky was killed in 1997 is nothing short of a travesty. The day when justice does not have to be fought for decades by traumatised and heartbroken families seems a long way off. This serves to remind us just how important is campaigning against racism, so we can look forward to day when there are no racist attacks, but if they do happen, justice is straightforwardly served, so families are left to simply grieve the loss of their loved one and somehow continue their life—a task that is hard enough in itself.

Dave Smith
Blacklist Support Group

I never knew Ricky Reel in person, but I first heard his name back in 1997, when I was given a leaflet at an anti-racism protest somewhere in London.

Ricky was a young Asian student who had lost his life on a night out in Kingston upon Thames after being attacked by a gang of racists. Ricky's tragic death was on the TV news, where journalists reported him as a statistic in a wave of racist violence against young Black and Asian men, which coincided with the rise of the British National Party.

What made Ricky so much more than a statistic to me, was when I saw his mother, Sukhdev Reel, speak about her son. Listening to a mother's grief for a murdered son is almost unbearable to watch, anyone with an ounce of humanity would be moved. But listening to Sukhdev talk about the shameful treatment her family received from the police at a time when they most needed support, made me seethe with anger.

I was heavily involved in campaigning against the British National Party and other racist groups who were stirring up hate and violence. Where the fascists tried to divide people, we brought our communities together; through trade unions, through music, through sharing our collective stories. Throughout this time, I continued to read articles about Ricky Reel, including at the times of the inquest into his death.

Over a decade later, the press broke the story about undercover police spying on people campaigning for a better world. The appalling news stories of undercover officers sexually abusing women activists and spying on Doreen and Neville Lawrence, who were fighting for justice on behalf of their son Stephen, outraged the nation.

As more of the long-hidden evidence was uncovered, it became clear that the Lawrence family were not the only grieving parents who were targeted by undercover police. Sukhdev and her family were also spied upon. At the very time that supporters, including their MP, were calling for police resources to find Ricky and afterwards his killers, the police instead sent undercover officers to spy on the Reel family. The police should hang their heads in shame at the appalling human rights violation of a grieving family.

I was also kept under surveillance by the UK political policing units because of my trade union and anti-fascist campaigning. I have met and spoken alongside Sukhdev many times; at conferences, in Parliament, at the Spy Cops public inquiry and at protests outside Scotland Yard. Sukhdev is an inspiration to all who meet her, and it is my honour to call her a friend and comrade in the struggle for justice. Like thousands of others who never knew Ricky in person, I came to know him as an intelligent, articulate, caring young man through the decades-long justice campaign led by his family.

Sukhdev Reel's book will allow many more people to learn about her son Ricky, but it is also a continuation of her tireless campaigning work since the 1990s. The book documents a tragic episode in one family's history; but is also a searing indictment of the institutional racism that runs through the Metropolitan Police and the British legal system from top to bottom. This is the kind of story that doesn't get taught in schools, but it should be mandatory for anyone who wants to understand the society we live in.

Neil Armstrong
Producer/Director/Lecturer

Sukhdev is tireless, driven and an absolute inspiration. Her fight for justice is both inspirational and humbling. I'm in awe of her.

Phil Chamberlain

I am angry: How can it be that a young man can disappear and the police do nothing to properly investigate? Indeed, that they would spy upon the family and supporters who are demanding simple justice? I am ashamed: That for all the fine words from those in authority Ricky Reel's supporters and family are still battling for answers. How can my neighbours be treated this way? I am in awe: Each time I have heard Sukhdev or supporters speak or read about the latest stage of the campaign. To simply refuse to be cowed. To challenge official incompetence and racism in a thousand different ways. To build a coalition of people who will not let this go. To fight, be pushed back but fight on. I am hopeful: Ricky's family will have justice. We will not accept any other outcome.

Anthony Way

I met Sukhdev in the 1990s through working at Hounslow Homeless Persons Unit. We sat opposite each other, paired for duties and shared daily working life. Our lives changed when Sukhdev's son Ricky went missing. We searched the streets for him, calling out his name, during the day, evenings, every available moment. It was harrowing. I took a shattering call at work from Suresh Grover informing us that Ricky's body had been found in the river Thames. Formal police investigations were inconclusive, lacked any strength or depth. Sukhdev's search for justice and closure on what happened to Ricky continues to this day. Revelations that police resources were used to spy on the family and supporters rather than on finding Ricky's killers further exacerbated the pain and suffering Sukhdev and her family have endured. An injustice of this proportion must be rectified.

Injustice anywhere is a threat to justice everywhere. Sukhdev and her family deserve justice. And Peace.

Bruce McDonald

For someone I never met, Ricky Reel has made a huge impression on my life.

No-one could be unmoved by the story of his tragic death and the callous indifference his family and their supporters experienced when he went missing. That was compounded by the obdurate refusal to investigate seriously.

What I learned from working with Sukhdev, Suresh and the Campaign confirmed me as an uncompromising advocate for racial justice. The experience influenced everything I did in my role as Chief Executive of the Royal Borough of Kingston.

The story begins in 1999, when I became Acting Chief Executive at Kingston. Relations between the Campaign and the Council were poor. There had been a demonstration outside the police station: "Kingston Police are racist police". I decided something needed to be done and offered a meeting. I was invited to the Monitoring Group's offices in Southall.

The reception surprised me. As soon as I had sat down, I was asked to sort out a concert for Ricky—scheduled for the following Saturday and threatened with cancellation. The University—the planned venue—had just withdrawn its agreement to the event taking place.

The Campaign would like the concert to be held at the Guildhall instead. Could I arrange it please?

I had been expecting to begin a discussion on ways to mark Ricky's memory but I knew instinctively that I had to help— to build trust. I wasn't sure how I was going to do it. At that point there was a Conservative Minority Administration of a No Overall Control Council. I was pretty sure that the idea of a concert at the Guildhall would not meet with universal acclaim.

The prudent move was to say no.

However, I knew instinctively that I had to help. So, I said yes, and we made the concert happen.

The next—and much more substantive—step was to arrange a memorial to Ricky and to establish a series of annual lectures. It was important that this was done in a way which showed that the Council was putting its whole weight behind the tribute. The Council's hosting of the lectures was both a mark of respect of the Reel family for their loss, and support for the cause of racial justice.

The right thing to do was to say yes. So I did. The Reel family had suffered so much hurt. We had to recognise that and show we stood with them in their time of need. It was a decision made on instinct. I knew I would be taking some in Kingston into a venture which would test them. The cautious choice would have been to be tentative. However, the family needed more than that and that dictated my response.

Importantly, everyone in Kingston, with a few initial hesitations, followed the lead; which is because when they came to understand what Sukhdev and her family were experiencing they responded with compassion. That, in turn, made the lectures achieve a powerful effect by both showing proper respect to the family for their loss but also deepening understanding of racial justice.

One story makes exactly that point. Before the first memorial lecture, a small group of us met in the Mayor's Parlour prior to unveiling the plaque to Ricky at the Guildhall. One of Suresh's requests had been that the lecture would be hosted by the Mayor, who was a very traditional Conservative. It took several meetings to persuade her. In particular, she was preoccupied about how she would explain to her friends that Mike Mansfield QC had been a guest in the parlour. Her sense of duty prevailed but it did not go so far as for her to be comfortable with the words "racial justice", which I had included in her speech. She crossed them out.

On the night itself, the reception in the parlour went well. We assembled by the plaque to Ricky. Sukhdev said a few words and read a poem. The Mayor asked me to go back to the parlour with her. We sat down. She had been very moved by what Sukhdev had said. She took out her fountain pen. Everywhere she had crossed out "racial justice" in her speech, she put it back in.

In her eyes that was a huge thing to do. It was her response as a mother to Sukhdev. I think she understood totally that no mother should ever have had to suffer what you had and she wanted to stand with you.

I tell that story now because it underlines the power that Sukhdev Reel, and her telling of Ricky's story, has to change the way people think.

I believe that Ricky would be very proud of the way his mother has used her strength to challenge prejudice, preconceptions and fight for justice. I am proud to have played a small part in supporting her.

Tommy Nagra,
Executive Director of Content at BBC

It's a privilege for me to be in your book and I very much hope you and the family are well. The television documentary, *The Reel Mystery*, broadcast on the BBC in 1997 is one that continues to resonate for many reasons. On a professional level it was the very first documentary that I made as a young, rookie Director, and whilst I have produced many hundreds since this film transmitted, it remains a regret that it asked more questions than sadly provide any answers. 25 years on, Sukhdev's quest for answers and justice has remained and I cannot imagine how challenging the years have been.

On a personal level, I was drawn to this story at a time when very little was being written about it. I first met Sukhdev and her family when they were grieving the loss of Ricky. The emotion was raw but Sukhdev's determination to find out how her son died was palpable and inspirational. I felt a strong urge to help tell her story and help her family find the answers to give them, at the very least, some form of closure.

As part of the documentary I interviewed the Reel family, campaigners, lawyers, the police, pathologists and the friends who were with Ricky on that fateful night. We staged a reconstruction using actors in the hope that somebody would step forward with more information. It is heartbreaking that almost a quarter of a century later the Reel family are still seeking answers as to how their beloved son was found at the bottom of a river after being racially abused.

Sukhdev's strength, resilience and humanity have remained resolute in the intervening years. Losing a child is every parent's worst nightmare . Not knowing what actually happened is beyond comprehension.

Hugh Goodacre

Reading Sukhdev's account of the terrible days following Ricky's disappearance has brought back memories of her incredible bravery and persistence in gaining justice for her son. At that time, I had been organising events of international and anti-racist solidarity, along with many others including Suresh and John McDonnell, and I was deeply impressed that Sukhdev was prepared to stand up publicly at these and many other events and share the unbelievable suffering of her recent bereavement with all others who had suffered such grief and injustice. To think that she has sustained this struggle in all the years since then displays a heart that is not only courageous, but utterly selfless and deeply generous. This book will play a powerful role in preserving the memory of her struggle for generations to come.

AB

I have known Sukhdev Reel since 1991 through my job. Since then we have become good friends. She is a very calm and collected person. A genuinely kind hearted, soft spoken and gentle human being. I remember when I heard about her son going missing one night on 14 October 1997 and due to the police not doing enough to find her son, a candlelit vigil took place in Kingston upon Thames. I took part in this march along with many others e.g. family, friends, Unison members & Hounslow Council employees.

All these years I have seen Sukhdev fighting for justice for her son, which has taken a toll on her health, whilst keeping herself mentally strong and determined. She has gone through a major surgery, which I believe is due to the stress linked to her fight for justice for Ricky's death. At times I felt her fight for justice was damaging her health. At the same time, I do realise, deep down she is a mother who would not give up and will fight until her last breath to get justice for Ricky, who was innocent and vulnerable and became a victim to a racist attack. Sukhdev's fight will carry on as she feels the police and detectives have either failed or ignored her son's case. Sukhdev, keep faith in almighty God and justice will be done to your son's death and your fight for justice will not go wasted.

Denis Fernando

I have been honoured to know and work with Sukhdev Reel and her family in their campaign for justice for over 20 years. I first came to know Sukhdev as a student activist at Goldsmiths College, where I was a student union officer and an activist of the Student Assembly Against Racism and the National Black Students Alliance. As student campaigners, we supported the families of Stephen Lawrence and Ricky Reel in their fight for justice, and campaigned to bring students to their campaign demands. The cases of Stephen Lawrence and Ricky Reel demonstrated that young people are the victims and perpetrators of racism in its most violent manifestations. Both were students, and were killed by young people.

Hearing Sukhdev speak was always a very powerful and emotional experience that hit me personally. I could hear the heartbreaking worry in her voice as she relived the night that Ricky did not return home. I had heard that worry in my own parents' voices if ever myself or my brothers were getting late home or were out of an evening. My parents' generation had come to Britain for a better life but were now facing a reality where racism was impacting on their lives and those of their children. I was always committed to supporting the Justice for Ricky Reel Campaign, because an Asian man of about the same age, he could have been me. Or one of my friends. The attitude of the police in those early days when he was missing disgusted me. That the family had to search for him unaided must have been horrific.

At the turn of the millennium I was elected as the NUS Black Students Officer. This position was created to represent students of African, Arab, Asian and Caribbean descent in the NUS because of the commitment of anti-racist student activists to bring the reality of the racism that Black students face into the NUS. We highlighted the cases of Stephen Lawrence and Ricky Reel to show how racism could impact on students of African, Arab, Asian and Caribbean descent. The position was a representative voice created for Black students nationally. I gave the proposing speech to create the position and referenced Stephen and Ricky. It was passed overwhelmingly.

After finishing at NUS, I continued anti-racism activism with the National Assembly Against Racism. Over the next 20 years, I would continue to support Sukhdev's family at conferences, demonstrations and often outside Scotland Yard. I was always struck at how Sukhdev would personally greet me at these events, even though she must have had so much on her mind at the time.

With Denis Fernando, NUS Black Students Officer, 2002

We became Facebook friends and I remember a few years back facetiously posting a status on my page from a joke I had read: "Don't burden your friends with your troubles...tell them to your enemies, who will be much happier to hear them". Sukhdev was one of my friends who liked the status. I was struck at how much courage it must take to carry on with any semblance of normality after losing a child in the way that she had. I was also struck at what the full meaning of her "troubles" would have been in partaking in this joke. Her troubles were much deeper and more painful than most will ever know. And yet here was Sukhdev, joining in with my joke and exhibiting a deep resilience and courage that inspires so many to this day.

And I do not talk of being inspired by Sukhdev lightly.

Tragically in 2020 my younger brother took his own life after decades of living with mental illness. This devastated my family and left us in a state of emotional freefall just as Covid shut down and isolated us from the support we so desperately needed to help us through what was the worst trauma of my life. Upon hearing of my loss, Sukhdev took the time to message me and call me, offering her own insights into her professional experience of caring for people with mental illness. It meant something unquantifiable to have the comforting words of someone like Sukhdev who has been through so much and yet was so deeply empathetic to the loss, anger, disbelief and shock that I was feeling every day. She had a deep understanding of the loss I was feeling and gave heartfelt regards to my family, that she had never met. She knew they would be in pain and that it would mean something to them.

Sukhdev is an unbelievably courageous campaigner. I think it must take a lot of strength to let people into the pain that you feel when an injustice happens and there is no closure. I think Ricky's case shows that there is still a long way to go in tackling institutional racism in institutions like the police. We all have to challenge racism to prevent the propagation of a society where people like Ricky can be killed due to the colour of his skin, and that can also mean his murder is treated as that of a second-class citizen. And anyone doubting that this is a priority need only look at the devastating impact that it had on a close knit family like his. It is critical that his family is given justice. Justice delayed and denied only makes the pain of losing a loved one in a racist murder all the more unbearable. I know now from my own personal loss, how important it is to ensure that Ricky is not forgotten. Sukhdev always remembers him, his bedroom was left untouched after he died. We can all do something to support this family by being a part of their campaign for justice.

Geoff Gill

I first met Sukhdev Reel when I came to work with her, in 2001, as a colleague in a local authority housing department. I knew from press reporting of the tragic loss of her beloved son Ricky—and I confess I was a little nervous when the subject of Ricky first came up in our informal conversations, as we got to know one another. I needn't have worried. Sukhdev is such a warm, wise and friendly person and she positively wanted me—and indeed the World—to know all about her beautiful, loving and gifted son. As Sukhdev and I became friends, I realised what a calm, sensitive and courageous woman she truly is—characteristics clearly also inherited by Ricky in how he lived his own life, so tragically cut short, but bursting with promise and lived to the full.

As a parent I have to say I cannot begin to imagine what Sukhdev and her family have had to endure, losing their cherished son and brother Ricky. All of the Reel family have borne their sorrows not only with the utmost dignity and positivity but also with a determination to fight for justice and truth. And their fight has not just been for Ricky but for sadly, too many other families who have also been faced with such an unbearable loss, only to encounter indifference, incompetence and even suspicion and invasion of privacy by the police and other authorities.

Institutional racism, illegal spying on the family by the security services, as well as unforgivable procedural failings and incompetence—the Reel family suffered them all in the wake of the terrible tragedy of Ricky's loss. But paradoxically these assaults have only served to make the family all the more determined that Ricky Reel will not only be fondly remembered by those who knew and loved him, but also that his own life and spirit will be admired as an inspiration—indeed more than that, as an undying beacon of hope to all those fighting for justice and truth, and opposing the ignorance and inhumanity of racism and inequality.

AN

I have had the pleasure of getting to know Sukhdev over the last 25 years and we have become close friends. Throughout the years she has continued to demonstrate a unique sincerity and calmness regardless of the situation.

Despite the difficulties she has faced in her life, she remains determined to seek justice for many causes close to her heart. Sukhdev firmly believes in equality and fairness for all. She is also devoted to supporting and empowering women who have suffered domestic violence.

To those around her, she is an inspirational woman. We hope she gets justice for her son. She is a reminder to us all that we cannot remain silent in the face of injustice.

Fariddah Cook

I have known Sukhdev as a work colleague and as a friend. The pain that a mother like Sukhdev goes through every single day is something I do not wish upon anyone.

This book is about a mother's struggle to get justice for her son and a tribute to his memories. It is written with the hope and optimism that justice for Ricky will one day prevail; a mother's fight to get answers from the Metropolitan Police amidst the very challenging barriers that have come her way.

I pray and hope this book will in some way open up the many answers that a mother wishes to know with the ultimate hope of obtaining the justice that Ricky rightly deserves.

Arun Kundnani

After the Macpherson Inquiry's report into institutional racism in the police was published in 1999, some of us worked to establish a broader movement to challenge structural racist violence—from the treatment of asylum seekers to deaths in prisons. The Lawrence family had campaigned for years against the police's failure to investigate the racist murder of their son Stephen, forcing the incoming Labour government to concede to a public inquiry in 1997. By 1999, we had become familiar with dozens of families, from every part of England, who had lost loved ones to racist violence. We learned how, like with the Lawrences, the tragedy of their losses was compounded by indifferent police forces failing to investigate, forcing grieving family members to become campaigners for justice.

I first met Sukhdev Reel that year too. Two years earlier her son Ricky, then aged 20, had been out with friends in Kingston. They were attacked and racially abused. They ran in different directions. Ricky was the only one who did not come home. Following the stereotype, the police initially pursued the theory that Ricky had run off to avoid an arranged marriage. Then Ricky's body was found in the Thames. The police suggested he must have fallen in the river by accident while urinating. To us, the circumstances of Ricky's death were reminiscent of Stephen Lawrence's. Like the Lawrences, the Reel family, led by Sukhdev, began to campaign. Over the following years, I saw Sukhdev speak many times at public meetings and demonstrations. I saw her interviewed on television news programmes I chanted with her at protests outside Scotland Yard. Her pain was palpable; so too was her strength. She persevered in her campaign in the face of obstacle after obstacle. Her aim was to learn the truth of what had happened to her son. In pursuing that goal, she became a leading voice pointing to the institutional racism of the police. We did not know at the time that, like the Lawrences, she was being spied on by the very police force that had failed to properly investigate her son's death. But Ricky's death signaled more than institutional racism in the police. The theory was that bringing to the fore a glossy consumerist multiculturalism would somehow weaken the structures of institutional racism. Ricky Reel's death was a reminder, if one were needed, that such an approach to anti-racism was flawed.

The Macpherson Inquiry's official recognition of institutional racism has long been forgotten. Sukhdev Reel's long-standing campaign serves to remind us what the term implies in practice: a police force that fails to properly investigate racist crimes, stereotypes victims' families, spies on its critics, and covers for itself. Sukhdev Reel continues her struggle. Like the mothers of the disappeared in Argentina's dirty war, she will not give up fighting to learn the truth of what happened to her son. And we must not give up on her.

Gursharan Lall

Sukhdev Reel: A loud voice….Power of pen and paper… in the hands of a rider. Sukhdev Reel: seated in the riding chariot, carrying the message of inspiration, strength, armed with strong self-belief and faith, standing firm with the true inner voice is surely a message clear and loud, never to give up in front of lies!!

I haven't read your book yet, but I can already sense that it will be so worth reading for all ages from young to old…

As it will be a tool for empowerment an aid to weaken and eradicate the evil, in whatever form it may be. Not ever, to let yourself exchange your life to live as a victim.

Reading the book will give empowerment in faith & strength for speaking.

The book will be a message of hope & courage to stand for truth that will continue making impact on many lives & many lives to come. Dear sis at the same time Tears & joy together!! What a dilemma?? God always is with you dear Sis

My best wishes & love.

Zarayna Pradyer

I first met Sukhdev Reel in the spring of 1999 at a public meeting in Kingston upon Thames, where she was appealing for help.

Why would this be? Parents who are grieving the loss of a child don't normally have to appear in public to ask for their help. And yet, this was the case with the Reel's late son, Ricky.

I listened with dismay to a recollection of apparent insensitivity, unawareness and uncouthness on the authorities' part leading to additional distress for the Reel family.

Worse, to my mind, was the perfunctory approach to investigating the suspicious death of Ricky Reel. If there was any enthusiasm, diligence or interest in this inquiry, the investigating authority seemed very skilled in hiding it.

Having offered what little help I could, I became a witness to the fact that the Reel family undertook as much of the investigation as they could. This appeared to be viewed, not as complementary to the official police inquiry, but as a rivalry: characteristic of all bureaucracies. My suspicions were upheld when we later discovered that the Justice for Ricky Reel Campaign had attracted the dishonourable attention of what has become known as the "Spy Cops" scandal. Yes, the family was investigated and spied upon. If only such resources and enthusiasm had been directed at the original inquiry into Ricky Reel's death.

During the last decades, I increasingly admired Mrs Reel's dedication to discovering the truth of Ricky's death, even when ill health impeded the Campaign. She has tirelessly leafletted, spoken at public meetings and on the media, contacted influencers, sought judicial advice and explored every avenue that might be helpful. Not only that, but she had been unfailingly ready to lend a sympathetic ear and helping hand to those who are buckling under similar burdens.

As I got to know the family, I was welcomed and treated with a generosity of spirit that tends to arise from those who have suffered. We have shared the most awful of stories but have also laughed at the ironies of life. I shall be forever grateful.

How nice it would have been to have known Ricky, who by now would undoubtedly have had a satisfying profession and a family. How bitter that realisation must be for the Reel family.

Unfortunately, we are still waiting for satisfactory answers to Ricky Reel's death, and hence the family are denied closure. I sincerely hope this book might provide that which the authorities were unable to.

Nevertheless, along with feelings of gratitude for the Reel family, my abiding conclusion is that suffering carves out a place in the heart where empathy and compassion can find shelter. God bless Mrs Reel and her family, and thank you.

NP

It is a huge honour to write a few words in this book in memory of Ricky Reel, by illustrating my observations at the time of his death. I was a work colleague of Ricky's courageous and inspirational mother Sukhdev Reel, when this heart breaking incident occurred. The whole workforce was stunned and shocked by what had happened. I remember so clearly Sukhdev returning to work to try to continue to support her young family financially, but she wasn't the same woman that we all had known and often heard laughing across the office floor. My words fall short in trying to describe the pain and emptiness in this mother's eyes. This was a woman who was a walking skeleton with numbness in her whole body. She carried her son's photo on a badge each day, screaming internally and externally for justice for her son Ricky, which still continues today so sadly.

HS

From my perspective (the eldest grandchild), I find everything that's happened very emotional even though I never got the chance to meet uncle Ricky. I feel like I know him well from the memories and his story being passed onto all the grandchildren; especially with my mum often talking about her sadness due to missing her brother.

With the rest of the grandchildren being so young, they're not fully aware of everything in detail. However, the way they show so much concern and love towards Ricky is something very special. This has influenced me to take criminology A level to broaden my knowledge on the subject as I'm at a time in my life where I'm choosing my path and what career I want to pursue as I approach adulthood, and I find the experiences of what happened to my uncle regarding his death heavily influencing what I choose to do next.

Lowkey

Thank you so so much for your kind words Sukhdev. I am so sorry for your loss and the terrible abuse by the state you have been subjected to. Whatever I can do to help I will. I will keep in mind some ideas about how to deal with what happened to your boy artistically and keep you posted. Me and my friends were also chased by a racist gang in Kingston in 2001 and reading of your son reminded me of it. I send you nothing but love and respect and truly appreciate your message.

Thank you Sukhdev, I saw some of your beautiful poetry for Ricky in the comments on that song, which really moved me and brought me to tears. You and the whole family are in our thoughts and prayers. We shall speak soon.

Break The Noise Records
"Justice for Ricky Reel"

Rishi Rich and *Eastenders* and *Bend It Like Beckham* **star, Ameet Chana** has teamed up with West London born Bollywood music producer **Rishi Rich** and singer-songwriter **Kiranee** to remind the world, through music, about the injustice faced by the family of Ricky Reel.

"Justice for Ricky Reel" is the emotive retelling, through song and the spoken word, of the true story of a mother and her continuous struggle for justice following the death of her beloved son. Ricky's mother, Sukhdev, resumed writing poetry after Ricky's death and those same words are sung by Kiranee in this dedication to Ricky's life. With Ameet Chana writing and performing the spoken word portions of this song; "Justice For Ricky Reel" is a true tale of every mother's worst nightmare and a reminder to stand up for what is right, despite the adversities we may face.

Excerpts of Sukhdev's interviews have been used within the track to highlight the obstacles her family have faced whilst raising questions into Ricky's death. Rishi Rich has put this project together from the heart to give Sukhdev Reel, a fighter and a mother, a voice of strength with the hope that the name Ricky Reel and the search for justice are not forgotten.

Actor, director and radio presenter **Ameet Chana** adds: "For young Asians growing up back in 1997, we all felt an immense sense of anger and injustice after Ricky's death. I can only pray that 24 years on, the police and the judicial system take this as an opportunity to right another wrong in the community."

Rishi Rich, Music Producer said: "People across the whole world know about Stephen Lawrence and the institutional racism that has been highlighted as a result of Doreen Lawrence's resolute determination for justice. However, Ricky's death happened three years later and the treatment his mother received was unforgivable. I was pretty much the same age as Ricky—and I remember everything about that time. Ricky's death and his mother's fight had a huge impact on me and this track is a tribute to both Ricky and his mother."

The supporting video is a simple tribute to Ricky Reel with family footage, his photos and images of various protests, marches and gatherings arranged by Sukhdev Reel over the last 20+ years. The emotional visual also includes Ameet Chana and Kiranee performing their portions of the track "Justice for Ricky Reel".

Kiranee Singer, song writer & producer said "Sukhdev's strength and resilience should be an inspiration to every woman out there. She has fought tooth and nail for answers, closure and justice and continues to do so. I sincerely hope that our song reminds people of what happened to Ricky and that the road to justice is still being travelled."

Raj Ghai, a Director of Media Moguls also assisted in the above project and arranged public meetings to highlight this case.

Sanj—Xzecutive "Ricky Reel is no more but he still lives in the hearts of many, especially his family who have gone through so many tribulations. Time may have passed but the Justice for Ricky Reel Campaign is still alive and kicking. Secrets do not always remain underground, just like worms they slowly emerge for the world to see. One day you worm/s will be exposed.

Aniruddha Das
Formerly known as "Dr Das," co-founder of Asian Dub Foundation

When we were asked by Sukhdev in 1997 to contribute a piece of music to a CD thatwould help promote the Justice 4 Ricky Reel Campaign, we didn't hesitate to say yes. Each member of Asian Dub Foundation had at various points in their lives been personally affected by racial abuse or violence.

We created the track "Promise 2 Ricky", and one or two benefits for the Justice 4 Ricky Campaign.

Over the years, we nevertheless monitored Sukhdev's struggle for justice for her son. The failings and "mistakes" of the police are well documented. To anyone with any level of intuition, especially those of us of colour, brought up in the '70s, the racial connotations of the case were glaringly obvious. It has always been bizarre to me that the police in TV dramas can solve cases with the slightest of clues, whereas their real-life counterparts are so hapless. Could it be that part of the police budget goes towards sponsoring screenwriters and actors to deliver an on-screen image of them as heroes, as talented, as compassionate, as a force for good? Ricky's family's experience found the police to be quite the opposite—institutionally incompetent, institutionally lazy, institutionally indifferent, institutionally complacent, institutionally lacking in tact and empathy. Either these—or institutionally racist.

With the disclosure in recent years that the Special Demonstration Squad were spying on Sukhdev and her family, adding yet more to their collective pain, we see an organisation that is also institutionally incapable of being held to account for its actions and inactions and institutionally petulant.

I understand Sukhdev's need to disseminate her story. Her courage and tenacity will be an inspiration to those engaged in similar such struggles and render insights into possible practical strategies. It will also confront the complacency of those of us who think things here have actually changed for the better.

Inspired by having worked with political poets, I decided it would be good to make use of actual spoken words from Sukhdev, so we recorded and sampled her voice. However, we underpinned these with typical ADF bass and drum loops to add a dub militancy to consolidate Sukhdev's resolute message of intent to get justice. We were to use this kind of sonic and textual template a number of times over the next few years, but here it was in its initial raw form.

Aniruddha Das and Asian Dub Foundation

Shaista Aziz
Journalist and lifelong anti-racism and equalities campaigner.

I was working at the *Eastern Eye* newspaper in my first proper full-time job as a journalist starting out my career when I first heard about the case of Ricky Reel. I started delving deeper into the circumstances surrounding his disappearance and his body being found in the River Thames in October 1997 following an altercation with two white youths who had racially abused and attacked a group of young Asian men, reportedly telling them "Paki's go home". Ricky was part of the group of Asian men who were set upon. As his friends fought the men off, Ricky disappeared, his body was found in the Thames a week later.

I couldn't shake the image of Ricky off and the image of his devastated and distraught mother, Sukhdev Reel, who had launched a public campaign to get to the truth about what had happened to her son. A softly spoken, calm and deeply dignified woman, Sukhdev went into battle with the might of the Metropolitan Police, with its racist and disrespectful police culture, and sections of the British media briefing against her and her Campaign for justice for her son. The more I read about Sukhdev and Ricky, the more I knew that I needed to get involved in the Campaign and work with the family to amplify their voices and their demand for justice.

Twenty-five years after her son's disappearance and his body being retrieved from the River Thames, Sukhdev Reel continues to fight for answers and justice for her son, Ricky. I remain in awe of her and her family's dignity, strength and resolve to get to the truth, despite the deep racist harm that has been inflicted upon them and the treatment they've received from the Metropolitan Police, which has included a report outlining how the Met's now disbanded undercover unit, the Special Demonstration Squad (SDS), had been spying on Sukhdev Reel. This revelation was made in 2014, but it was something that those close to Sukhdev and campaigning with her including me were long suspicious of.

I went to visit Sukhdev early on at her home in a small village close to Heathrow Airport. I vividly remember meeting Sukhdev for the first time. She was sitting on the edge of her sofa and in her lap were several files full of newspaper cuttings about Ricky and paperwork related to his case. On the walls of her living room there were framed photographs of her son Ricky and the many sporting trophies he had won during his short life. Ricky's dad came to greet us. I was there with my colleague Ushma Vyas, a fellow reporter at the *Eastern Eye*. We sat and listened to Sukhdev. She explained in great detail her fight to get answers about what had happened to Ricky and how her son's unexplained death was tormenting her. I sensed strongly that Sukhdev—whose name translates as a person who provides peace, brings peace—had in fact had all her peace, joy and reason for living snatched away from her cruelly the evening her son vanished and was returned to her in a coffin.

Sukhdev and her family deserve all the peace in the world, and I hope, inshallah, one day that alongside finding justice for her son, Ricky, Sukhdev is granted peace too.

Following our first meeting, I became part of the Justice for Ricky Reel Campaign and would speak to Sukhdev at least once a week. I ensured that the *Eastern Eye* published regular updates on the Campaign for justice and met with the tireless and legendary anti-racism campaigner, and founder of the Southall Monitoring Group, set up to investigate cases of racism across London and the UK and support victims' families. Suresh Grover was and remains one of the Reel family's main supporters to this day. I also had regular meetings with Imran Khan, who had also represented Stephen Lawrence's family in their long battle for justice for their son Stephen Lawrence, which accumulated in the publishing of the Macpherson Report, slamming the Metropolitan Police for being institutionally racist. I also meet the man who wasthe Reel family's MP and has remained steadfast and unwavering in his support of

Sukhdev and her family, John McDonnell MP.

As young women reporters at the *Eastern Eye* newspaper, Ushma and I decided to make sure we did everything in our personal and professional power to support Sukhdev Reel and her family. We knew that we could bring several prominent and well-known British Asian artists together in the field of music, acting and popular culture and mobilise them to join the Campaign to demand justice for Ricky. We opened up our contacts book and called in favours. We got flyers and leaflets printed, we mobilised high-profile Asian musicians who agreed to play at a fundraising gig in Kingston upon Thames, where Ricky's body was found, as an act of solidarity and to bring members of the British South Asian community together to put pressure on the police, government and authorities to investigate what had happened to Ricky and to provide answers over how he had died.

We decided to name the tribute to Ricky and the musical evening "Keeping it Reel"—Justice for Ricky Reel. Ushma and I coordinated over the flyers to be distributed across London and outside Bhangra and desi clubs in the city. We convinced musician's, DJs and artists to wear t-shirts with Ricky's name and face on and to talk about Ricky when they were publicising their music and gigs. Every artist we contacted came back to us with a positive response. We were often asked by musician's why wasn't Ricky's case headline news and why wasn't there more mass outrage about the serious questions remaining unanswered about how Ricky died and why the police had been so disrespectful to his family and applied a number or racist stereotypes to Ricky's case from day one of the police investigation. We found that we couldn't provide answers to these questions but what we did do was continue to mobilise and build the Campaign for justice with Sukhdev, the family, Suresh, and John.

The Keep It Reel event was a success—we secured TV, broadcast and print media coverage and we had connected the family campaign with leading British Asian artists. It was the start of wider consciousness raising and of ensuring the British South Asian community, and especially younger people, people around Ricky's age when his life was cruelly snatched from him, understand and know Ricky's story and his family's story is part of a wider and collective story of racial justice for all our communities and people and communities of colour in our country. And it is also about ensuring there is redress and accountability in relation to the Metropolitan Police and their treatment of Ricky's family and ongoing institutional racism in the police force.

Twenty-five years on from the launch of the Justice for Ricky Reel Campaign and there is still no justice for Ricky, his mother Sukhdev or his wider family. The world is much changed and, in many ways, an even more broken place when it comes to the struggle for racial justice. The issue of racism in all its forms including institutional racism in all our institutions and places and our places of learning and work continue to have a powerful light shine on them by campaigners and activists—most recently by the global Black Lives Matter movement. Politically, in the UK, the daily gaslighting and denial of everyday and structural racism has peaked over the past few years—but at the same time more and more people are understanding that Britain needs a deep and uncomfortable reckoning over how race, racism, institutional and structural racism, shapes the experiences and life chances of so many British people and communities. It is through the tenacity, courage, fight and struggle of women and mothers such as Sukhdev Reel and Doreen Lawrence that these failures are being exposed and change is taking place—the personal and life cost of course is too high. Society must ensure there is justice for Ricky and for all victims of racist violence and racist police indifference.

Su Goodacre
Author of 'Far Too Dangerous'

You know something, so "man-up".

You've fought the fight for denial, but your power is invisible, overshadowed by the corner you are trapped in.

While straddling the turnstile of weakness you can be within touching distance of greatness—but only once you have smashed against your own machine. When you admit the nation you guard is powerless in its defensiveness.

The pain of your gutlessness is soothed once you disable machismo. You are vulnerable but, take on the challenge of that inner ugly deceitful truth. Guide fear to the surface. Then you can fly the flag.

Sukhdev has shown you strength. She has carried the mantle of warriors on her back for too long and would like to swap it with your shield. It's an easy exchange once you weigh your cowardice against your conscience and share your struggle.

You know her son because her son is every son.

Has dismantling the pride of the dead stood you in good stead?

To know dignity, you will dispense with the ego of an empire. Prepare to reveal how much you hate yourself—in the name of the love you will gain for yourself.

For the relief of rectitude. Lay your lies on the line.

We will meet you at the frontier.

Jagdish Patel

I first met Sukhdev Reel and Ricky's family only a few days after he disappeared in October 1997. After work, I would volunteer with the team at then Southall Monitoring Group to go to Kingston town centre, walk the streets and hand out leaflets. The family loved Ricky, and knew his disappearance was out of character, but even when, in their terrible state of trauma, they tried to communicate this to the official body tasked with resources to help, they were still treated as suspects.

As the Campaign developed Sukhdev talked about her experiences everywhere, and I would often after work, drive her and Neville Lawrence to different places across London and the Southeast to talk to crowds of people about their experiences. Both spoke humbly from their hearts about their cases, and its impact. This left impact on others, but what it did to them having to repeat this night after night, I don't know.

As the Campaign for justice developed, and Neville Lawrence would later launch the Campaign, as its shortcoming mirrored so closely that of the family of Stephen Lawrence, the Reel family would be one of around 30 families who in the aftermath of the McPherson report would launch a broader campaign for justice for families, for family-led movements with a broad anti-racist ethos, bringing people from different backgrounds together. Although this was partly about structural changes, most importantly it was way to ensure that people facing the same issues were not isolated.

Sukhdev's voice, both as a mother who had successful raised and loved a son to his late teens, but also then traumatically lose him, was vital. She spoke and people listened, not just to someone who was a victim, but someone who cared deeply that the lessons could be learnt to avoid others facing the same trauma she had faced. She made her own agency, and she cared that her son, and her experiences would not be forgotten. In this way, she lives in the shadows of countless women from across the Globe who have led movements, in South America,

South Africa, South Asia, Middle East and the States. These women bring much to the struggles and have a lot to teach the anti-racist movement.

For the Police, the McPherson report termed the experiences of families as "secondary victimisation"—a process which reinforces and repeats the initial trauma faced by the victim. However, it is difficult to say if they really learnt any lessons when, twenty years later, we learn about the scale of the counter surveillance operation against the family, here just a simple family coping with grief. Now we really must evaluate where the suspicion which prevented the initial investigation, and started this campaign, takes us as a society, not only for its impact on the family, but also on the mindset of the police service and the soul of what they call intelligence. James Baldwin once said to a meeting in London when a mother spoke and talked about her son's experiences in Britain, 'listen to her, all of our futures are connected to her'. Hopefully this book will help us all.

Taranjit Chana
Chair of GMB Race

I have followed Sukhdev's journey from the time I heard her son, Ricky Reel, went missing to her long lonely fight for justice and answers to why his death was never properly investigated. As a black woman of south Asian heritage, Sukhdev's struggle for justice has been relentless, against the tide of racism crashing against her every move. It is time her story is heard, her voice amplified in her campaign for justice for Ricky . Her book will continue this fight.

Gary Calton

I first met Sukhdev at the launch of the National Civil Right movement at Camden Town Hall, London. She was speaking about the her son Ricky and the circumstance about his murder and the subsequent police investigations. Sukhdev agreed to take part in a documentary project I was working on: *Citizens of Our Time*. The project would go on to document 25 years of protester portraits with their own direct hand written message on the print. *Citizens of Our Time* exhibited at the Side Gallery, Newcastle 23 April to 26 June 2022.

Justice for Ricky Real
(11.7.77 – 15.10.99)

Holding you in my arms for the first time
Hearing you cry out loud
As the mother of the most perfect Son
I could not help but feel overwhelmingly proud.

From a baby to manhood
I watched you grow with pride
Thousands of responsibilities you
That you took quietly in your stride

Each moment of your life my son
I had dreamt & planned
So that now, in this darkness, it is hard for me
To accept your death and understand.

That all these dreams
Which together you and I Shared
The many hurdles yet to come in your life
For which you were prepared

You gave me love and happiness
For twenty memorable years
Free of pain & dismay
Free from all anxieties & fears.

All I have now to offer others
Is my aching heart
Since the pain of losing you, Ricky
To tearing your mother apart

There is one question I ask myself
Day after agonising day
How could mankind be so cruel
As to take such a young promising
life away

All my love my darling Ricky
Sukhdev Reel.

Thank you for reading my story

This is my own story
Written with a broken heart
From the grief, heartbreak, pain and sorrow
Of a life cruelly torn apart

I spend endless days campaigning
Reliving the moments, I hoped I forgot
Surrounded by anger, frustration and so much pain
Hoping the endless agony might somehow stop

Unable to turn my mind to contentment and peace
So I asked why was my son murdered that night?
Instead of getting answers or truth, or justice
Hurdles were thrown in the way of my plight

Without my family and the campaign's supporters
I would not have written this book this year
"Keep going" "we are with you", words meant so much to me
Kept me alive when I really wanted to disappear

This book belongs to everyone out there
Who has offered a kind word and stood by my side
Every time I fell on the floor or fainted
Lifted me up when I crumpled or cried

Too many people to thank for giving me strength
Their names alone would fill a book apart
But you know who you are, and what you have meant to me
And hold a special place in my heart

"Thank you"—the word seems so simple so small
For all the love and support you gave
Please know, that you kept me sane when I thought I was falling

You kept me strong, solid and brave

To the people who did wrong by me and mine
I say hatred is a very heavy weight
I bear no grudges or malice towards them
I won't be deviated from my path to justice, by hate

It is not in my nature to cause hurt or pain
Ricky became a friend to everyone he met
Thus his legacy of love and forgiveness is for you all
Live each day with love and no regrets

The road ahead is still dark, dearest Ricky
I don't know who killed you or why, that October night
But I will fight on till my last breath on this earth
Till I see you again, and can hold you so tight

From my fight I ask others to take courage and strength
If I can do it, you too can take a stand
Such fights for justice can only succeed
If we fight them arm in arm, hand in hand

Fight for something or someone you love and care for
Know there will be others fighting for the same
Know like me you are not alone in your struggles
Know that no struggle is ever in vain

Sleep peacefully my son. No one is going to hurt you again.
Sukhdev Reel, your mum

Endnotes

1 The full text of the Hansard Report of John McDonnell's speech can be found here: https://hansard.parliament.uk/commons/1999-10-20/debates/48d6bf57-4654-44ed-84c6-c782da1f4ba7/RickyReel

2 See Undercover Policing Inquiry website https://www.ucpi.org.uk/

3 Undercover Policing—Who is Involved, https://www.ucpi.org.uk/who-is-involved/

4 The opening statement is available here: *https://www.ucpi.org.uk/wp-content/uploads/2020/11/20201026-Opening_Statement_CPs_represented-by_HJA_BM_Bindmans-MRQC.pdf*

5 Theresa May's announcement about the Inquiry is here *https://www.gov.uk/government/news/home-secretary-announces-statutory-inquiry-into-undercover-policing*

6 Chair of the Inquiry's opening remarks are available here https://www.ucpi.org.uk/wp-content/uploads/2015/07/Opening-Remarks.pdf

7 Report of the Saville Iquiry into Bloody Sunday available here https://www.gonv.uk/government/publications/report-of-the-bloody-sunday-inquiry

8 Dean Jones, 2016, Fatal call: getting away w*ith murder: a study into influences of decision making at the initial scene of unexpected death*, PhD Thesis, School of Criminology and Criminal Justice, University of Portsmouth, p.26. https://researchportal.port.ac.uk/en/studentTheses/fatal-call-getting-away-with-murder

9 Hall, Nathan, Grieve, John & Savage, Stephen, 2009, *Policing and the Legacy of Lawrence,* (London: Routledge).

10 *Chapter 8 page 70, 177 & 178.*

11 *BBC News, 6 January 2000, 7.35am GMT.*

12 *An Oral History of the Runnymede Trust*, 1968-1988.